The Miser

MOLIERE

Contents

THE MISER

BY
MOLIERE

THE MISER. (L'AVARE.)
BY
MOLIERE

TRANSLATED INTO ENGLISH PROSE
BY
CHARLES HERON WALL

This play was acted for the first time on September 9, 1668. In it, Moliere has borrowed from Plautus, and has imitated several other authors, but he far surpasses them in the treatment of his subject. The picture of the miser, in whom love of money takes the place of all natural affections, who not only withdraws from family intercourse, but considers his children as natural enemies, is finely drawn, and renders Moliere's Miser altogether more dramatic and moral than those of his predecessors.

Moliere acted the part of Harpagon.

PERSONS REPRESENTED.

HARPAGON, CLEANTE, MARIANNE.
CLEANTE, HARPAGON'S MARIANNE.
VALERE, ANSELME, ELISE.
ANSELME, VALERE MARIANNE.
MASTER SIMON, .
MASTER JACQUES, HARPAGON.
LA FLECHE, CLEANTE.
BRINDAVOINE, and LA MERLUCHE, HARPAGON.
A MAGISTRATE CLERK.
ELISE, HARPAGON.
MARIANNE, ANSELME.
FROSINE, .
MISTRESS CLAUDE, HARPAGON.

*   *   *   *   *

PARIS, HARPAGON'S .

THE MISER.

ACT I.

SCENE I.--VALERE, ELISE.

VAL. What, dear Elise! you grow sad after having given me such dear
tokens of your love; and I see you sigh in the midst of my joy! Can
you regret having made me happy? and do you repent of the engagement
which my love has forced from you?

ELI. No, Valere, I do not regret what I do for you; I feel carried on
by too delightful a power, and I do not even wish that things should
be otherwise than they are. Yet, to tell you the truth, I am very
anxious about the consequences; and I greatly fear that I love you
more than I should.

VAL. What can you possibly fear from the affection you have shown me?

ELI. Everything; the anger of my father, the reproaches of my family,
the censure of the world, and, above all, Valere, a change in your
heart! I fear that cruel coldness with which your sex so often repays
the too warm proofs of an innocent love.

VAL. Alas! do not wrong me thus; do not judge of me by others. Think me capable of everything, Elise, except of falling short of what I owe to you. I love you too much for that; and my love will be as lasting as my life!

ELI. Ah! Valere, all men say the same thing; all men are alike in their words; their actions only show the difference that exists between them.

VAL. Then why not wait for actions, if by them alone you can judge of the truthfulness of my heart? Do not suffer your anxious fears to mislead you, and to wrong me. Do not let an unjust suspicion destroy the happiness which is to me dearer than life; but give me time to show you by a thousand proofs the sincerity of my affection.

ELI. Alas! how easily do we allow ourselves to be persuaded by those we love. I believe you, Valere; I feel sure that your heart is utterly incapable of deceiving me, that your love is sincere, and that you will ever remain faithful to me. I will no longer doubt that happiness is near. If I grieve, it will only be over the difficulties of our position, and the possible censures of the world.

VAL. But why even this fear?

ELI. Oh, Valere! if everybody knew you as I do, I should not have much to fear. I find in you enough to justify all I do for you; my heart knows all your merit, and feels, moreover, bound to you by deep gratitude. How can I forget that horrible moment when we met for the first time? Your generous courage in risking your own life to save mine from the fury of the waves; your tender care afterwards; your constant attentions and your ardent love, which neither time nor difficulties can lessen! For me you neglect your parents and your

country; you give up your own position in life to be a servant of my
father! How can I resist the influence that all this has over me? Is
it not enough to justify in my eyes my engagement to you? Yet, who
knows if it will be enough to justify it in the eyes of others? and
how can I feel sure that my motives will be understood?

VAL. You try in vain to find merit in what I have done; it is by my
love alone that I trust to deserve you. As for the scruples you feel,
your father himself justifies you but too much before the world; and
his avarice and the distant way in which he lives with his children
might authorise stranger things still. Forgive me, my dear Elise, for
speaking thus of your father before you; but you know that,
unfortunately, on this subject no good can be said of him. However, if
I can find my parents, as I fully hope I shall, they will soon be
favourable to us. I am expecting news of them with great impatience;
but if none comes I will go in search of them myself.

ELI. Oh no! Valere, do not leave me, I entreat you. Try rather to
ingratiate yourself in my father's favour.

VAL. You know how much I wish it, and you can see how I set about it.
You know the skilful manoeuvres I have had to use in order to
introduce myself into his service; under what a mask of sympathy and
conformity of tastes I disguise my own feelings to please him; and
what a part I play to acquire his affection. I succeed wonderfully
well, and I feel that to obtain favour with men, there are no better
means than to pretend to be of their way of thinking, to fall in with
their maxims, to praise their defects, and to applaud all their
doings. One need not fear to overdo it, for however gross the
flattery, the most cunning are easily duped; there is nothing so
impertinent or ridiculous which they will not believe, provided it be
well seasoned with praise. Honesty suffers, I acknowledge; but when we
have need of men, we may be allowed without blame to adapt ourselves

to their mode of thought; and if we have no other hope of success but through such stratagem, it is not after all the fault of those who flatter, but the fault of those who wish to be flattered.

ELI. Why do you not try also to gain my brother's goodwill, in case the servant should betray our secret?

VAL. I am afraid I cannot humour them both. The temper of the father is so different from that of the son that it would be difficult to be the confidant of both at the same time. Rather try your brother yourself; make use of the love that exists between you to enlist him in our cause. I leave you, for I see him coming. Speak to him, sound him, and see how far we can trust him.

ELI. I greatly fear I shall never have the courage to speak to him of my secret.

SCENE II.--CLEANTE, ELISE,

CLE. I am very glad to find you alone, sister. I longed to speak to you and to tell you a secret.

ELI. I am quite ready to hear you, brother. What is it you have to tell me?

CLE. Many things, sister, summed up in one word--love.

ELI. You love?

CLE. Yes, I love. But, before I say more, let me tell you that I know I depend on my father, and that the name of son subjects me to his will; that it would be wrong to engage ourselves without the consent of the authors of our being; that heaven has made them the masters of our affections, and that it is our duty not to dispose of ourselves but in accordance to their wish; that their judgment is not biassed by their being in love themselves; that they are, therefore, much more likely not to be deceived by appearances, and to judge better what is good for us; that we ought to trust their experience rather than the passion which blinds us; and that the rashness of youth often carries us to the very brink of dangerous abysses. I know all this, my sister, and I tell it you to spare you the trouble of saying it to me, for my love will not let me listen to anything, and I pray you to spare me your remonstrances.

ELI. Have you engaged yourself, brother, to her you love?

CLE. No, but I have determined to do so; and I beseech you once more not to bring forward any reason to dissuade me from it.

ELI. Am I such a very strange person, brother?

CLE. No, dear sister; but you do not love. You know not the sweet power that love has upon our hearts; and I dread your wisdom.

ELI. Alas! my brother, let us not speak of my wisdom. There are very few people in this world who do not lack wisdom, were it only once in their lifetime; and if I opened my heart to you, perhaps you would think me less wise than you are yourself.

CLE. Ah! would to heaven that your heart, like mine....

ELI. Let us speak of you first, and tell me whom it is you love.

CLE. A young girl who has lately come to live in our neighbourhood, and who seems made to inspire love in all those who behold her. Nature, my dear sister, has made nothing more lovely; and I felt another man the moment I saw her. Her name is Marianne, and she lives with a good, kind mother, who is almost always ill, and for whom the dear girl shows the greatest affection. She waits upon her, pities and comforts her with a tenderness that would touch you to the very soul. Whatever she undertakes is done in the most charming way; and in all her actions shine a wonderful grace, a most winning gentleness, an adorable modesty, a ... ah! my sister, how I wish you had but seen her.

ELI. I see many things in what you tell me, dear brother; and it is sufficient for me to know that you love her for me to understand what she is.

CLE. I have discovered, without their knowing it, that they are not in very good circumstances, and that, although they live with the greatest care, they have barely enough to cover their expenses. Can you imagine, my sister, what happiness it must be to improve the condition of those we love; skilfully to bring about some relief to the modest wants of a virtuous family? And think what grief it is for me to find myself deprived of this great joy through the avarice of a father, and for it to be impossible for me to give any proof of my love to her who is all in all to me.

ELI. Yes, I understand, dear brother, what sorrow this must be to you.

CLE. It is greater, my sister, than you can believe. For is there anything more cruel than this mean economy to which we are subjected? this strange penury in which we are made to pine? What good will it do us to have a fortune if it only comes to us when we are not able to enjoy it; if now to provide for my daily maintenance I get into debt on every side; if both you and I are reduced daily to beg the help of tradespeople in order to have decent clothes to wear? In short, I wanted to speak to you that you might help me to sound my father concerning my present feelings; and if I find him opposed to them, I am determined to go and live elsewhere with this most charming girl, and to make the best of what Providence offers us. I am trying everywhere to raise money for this purpose; and if your circumstances, dear sister, are like mine, and our father opposes us, let us both leave him, and free ourselves from the tyranny in which his hateful avarice has for so long held us.

ELI. It is but too true that every day he gives us more and more reason to regret the death of our mother, and that....

CLE. I hear his voice. Let us go a little farther and finish our talk.
We will afterwards join our forces to make a common attack on his hard
and unkind heart.

SCENE III.--HARPAGON, LA FLECHE.

HAR. Get out of here, this moment; and let me have no more of your prating. Now then, be gone out of my house, you sworn pickpocket, you veritable gallows' bird.

LA FL. (). I never saw anything more wicked than this cursed old man; and I truly believe, if I may be allowed to say so, that he is possessed with a devil.

HAR. What are you muttering there between your teeth?

LA FL. Why do you send me away?

HAR. You dare to ask me my reasons, you scoundrel? Out with you, this moment, before I give you a good thrashing.

LA FL. What have I done to you?

HAR. Done this, that I wish you to be off.

LA FL. My master, your son, gave me orders to wait for him.

HAR. Go and wait for him in the street, then; out with you; don't stay in my house, straight and stiff as a sentry, to observe what is going on, and to make your profit of everything. I won't always have before me a spy on all my affairs; a treacherous scamp, whose cursed eyes watch all my actions, covet all I possess, and ferret about in every corner to see if there is anything to steal.

LA FL. How the deuce could one steal anything from you? Are you a man likely to be robbed when you put every possible thing under lock and key, and mount guard day and night?

HAR. I will lock up whatever I think fit, and mount guard when and where I please. Did you ever see such spies as are set upon me to take note of everything I do? () I tremble for fear he should suspect something of my money. () Now, aren't you a fellow to give rise to stories about my having money hid in my house?

LA FL. You have some money hid in your house?

HAR. No, scoundrel! I do not say that. (Aside) I am furious! (Aloud) I only ask if out of mischief you do not spread abroad the report that I have some?

LA FL. Oh! What does it matter whether you have money, or whether you have not, since it is all the same to us?

HAR. (raising his hand to give LA FLECHE a blow). Oh! oh! You want to argue, do you? I will give you, and quickly too, some few of these arguments about your ears. Get out of the house, I tell you once more.

LA FL. Very well; very well. I am going.

HAR. No, wait; are you carrying anything away with you?

LA FL. What can I possibly carry away?

HAR. Come here, and let me see. Show me your hands.

LA FL. There they are.

HAR. The others.

LA FL. The others?

HAR. Yes.

LA FL. There they are.

HAR. (). Have you anything hid
in here?

LA FL. Look for yourself.

HAR. (). These wide knee-
breeches are convenient receptacles of stolen goods; and I wish a pair
of them had been hanged.

LA FL. (). Ah! how richly such a man deserves what he
fears, and what joy it would be to me to steal some of his....

HAR. Eh?

LA FL. What?

HAR. What is it you talk of stealing?

LA FL. I say that you feel about everywhere to see if I have been stealing anything.

HAR. And I mean to do so too. (He feels in LA FLECHE'S pockets).

LA FL. Plague take all misers and all miserly ways!

HAR. Eh? What do you say?

LA FL. What do I say?

HAR. Yes. What is it you say about misers and miserly ways.

LA FL. I say plague take all misers and all miserly ways.

HAR. Of whom do you speak?

LA FL. Of misers.

HAR. And who are they, these misers?

LA FL. Villains and stingy wretches!

HAR. But what do you mean by that?

LA FL. Why do you trouble yourself so much about what I say?

HAR. I trouble myself because I think it right to do so.

LA FL. Do you think I am speaking about you?

HAR. I think what I think; but I insist upon your telling me to whom you speak when you say that.

LA FL. To whom I speak? I am speaking to the inside of my hat.

HAR. And I will, perhaps, speak to the outside of your head.

LA FL. Would you prevent me from cursing misers?

HAR. No; but I will prevent you from prating and from being insolent. Hold your tongue, will you?

LA FL. I name nobody.

HAR. Another word, and I'll thrash you.

LA FL. He whom the cap fits, let him wear it.

HAR. Will you be silent?

LA FL. Yes; much against my will.

HAR. Ah! ah!

LA FL. (HARPAGON).
Just look, here is one more pocket. Are you satisfied?

HAR. Come, give it up to me without all that fuss.

LA FL. Give you what?

HAR. What you have stolen from me.

LA FL. I have stolen nothing at all from you.

HAR. Are you telling the truth?

LA FL. Yes.

HAR. Good-bye, then, and now you may go to the devil.

LA FL. (). That's a nice way of dismissing anyone.

HAR. I leave it to your conscience, remember!

SCENE IV.--HARPAGON (.)

This rascally valet is a constant vexation to me; and I hate the very sight of the good-for-nothing cripple. Really, it is no small anxiety to keep by one a large sum of money; and happy is the man who has all his cash well invested, and who needs not keep by him more than he wants for his daily expenses. I am not a little puzzled to find in the whole of this house a safe hiding-place. Don't speak to me of your strong boxes, I will never trust to them. Why, they are just the very things thieves set upon!

SCENE V.--HARPAGON;

ELISE and CLEANTE are seen talking together at
the back of the stage.

HAR. (.) Meanwhile, I hardly know whether
I did right to bury in my garden the ten thousand crowns which were
paid to me yesterday. Ten thousand crowns in gold is a sum
sufficiently.... (ELISE CLEANTE
) Good heavens! I have betrayed myself; my
warmth has carried me away. I believe I spoke aloud while reasoning
with myself. (CLEANTE ELISE) What do you want?

CLE. Nothing, father.

HAR. Have you been here long?

ELI. We have only just come.

HAR. Did you hear...?

CLE. What, father?

HAR. There...!

CLE. What?

HAR. What I was just now saying.

CLE. No.

HAR. You did. I know you did.

ELI. I beg your pardon, father, but we did not.

HAR. I see well enough that you overheard a few words. The fact is, I was only talking to myself about the trouble one has nowadays to raise any money; and I was saying that he is a fortunate man who has ten thousand crowns in his house.

CLE. We were afraid of coming near you, for fear of intruding.

HAR. I am very glad to tell you this, so that you may not misinterpret things, and imagine that I said that it was I who have ten thousand crowns.

CLE. We do not wish to interfere in your affairs.

HAR. Would that I had them, these ten thousand crowns!

CLE. I should not think that....

HAR. What a capital affair it would be for me.

CLE. There are things....

HAR. I greatly need them.

CLE. I fancy that....

HAR. It would suit me exceedingly well.

ELI. You are....

HAR. And I should not have to complain, as I do now, that the times are bad.

CLE. Dear me, father, you have no reason to complain; and everyone knows that you are well enough off.

HAR. How? I am well enough off! Those who say it are liars. Nothing can be more false; and they are scoundrels who spread such reports.

ELI. Don't be angry.

HAR. It is strange that my own children betray me and become my enemies.

CLE. Is it being your enemy to say that you have wealth?

HAR. Yes, it is. Such talk and your extravagant expenses will be the cause that some day thieves will come and cut my throat, in the belief that I am made of gold.

CLE. What extravagant expenses do I indulge in?

HAR. What! Is there anything more scandalous than this sumptuous attire with which you jaunt it about the town? I was remonstrating with your sister yesterday, but you are still worse. It cries vengeance to heaven; and were we to calculate all you are wearing, from head to foot, we should find enough for a good annuity. I have told you a hundred times, my son, that your manners displease me exceedingly; you affect the marquis terribly, and for you to be always dressed as you are, you must certainly rob me.

CLE. Rob you? And how?

HAR. How should I know? Where else could you find money enough to clothe yourself as you do?

CLE. I, father? I play; and as I am very lucky, I spend in clothes all the money I win.

HAR. It is very wrong. If you are lucky at play, you should profit by it, and place the money you win at decent interest, so that you may find it again some day. I should like to know, for instance, without mentioning the rest, what need there is for all these ribbons with which you are decked from head to foot, and if half a dozen tags are not sufficient to fasten your breeches. What necessity is there for anyone to spend money upon wigs, when we have hair of our own growth, which costs nothing. I will lay a wager that, in wigs and ribbons alone, there are certainly twenty pistoles spent, and twenty pistoles brings in at least eighteen livres six sous eight deniers per annum, at only eight per cent interest.

CLE. You are quite right.

HAR. Enough on this subject; let us talk of something else. (Aside, noticingandwho make signs to one another)
I believe they are making signs to one another to pick my pocket.
() What do you mean by those signs?

ELI. We are hesitating as to who shall speak first, for we both have something to tell you.

HAR. And I also have something to tell you both.

CLE. We wanted to speak to you about marriage, father.

HAR. The very thing I wish to speak to you about.

ELI. Ah! my father!

HAR. What is the meaning of that exclamation? Is it the word, daughter, or the thing itself that frightens you?

CLE. Marriage may frighten us both according to the way you take it; and our feelings may perhaps not coincide with your choice.

HAR. A little patience, if you please. You need not be alarmed. I know what is good for you both, and you will have no reason to complain of anything I intend to do. To begin at the beginning. (CLEANTE) Do you know, tell me, a young person, called Marianne, who lives not far from here?

CLE. Yes, father.

HAR. And you?

ELI. I have heard her spoken of.

HAR. Well, my son, and how do you like the girl?

CLE. She is very charming.

HAR. Her face?

CLE. Modest and intelligent.

HAR. Her air and manner?

CLE. Perfect, undoubtedly.

HAR. Do you not think that such a girl well deserves to be thought of?

CLE. Yes, father.

HAR. She would form a very desirable match?

CLE. Very desirable.

HAR. That there is every likelihood of her making a thrifty and careful wife.

CLE. Certainly.

HAR. And that a husband might live very happily with her?

CLE. I have not the least doubt about it.

HAR. There is one little difficulty; I am afraid she has not the fortune we might reasonably expect.

CLE. Oh, my father, riches are of little importance when one is sure of marrying a virtuous woman.

HAR. I beg your pardon. Only there is this to be said: that if we do not find as much money as we could wish, we may make it up in something else.

CLE. That follows as a matter of course.

HAR. Well, I must say that I am very much pleased to find that you entirely agree with me, for her modest manner and her gentleness have won my heart; and I have made up my mind to marry her, provided I find she has some dowry.

CLE. Eh!

HAR. What now?

CLE. You are resolved, you say...?

HAR. To marry Marianne.

CLE. Who? you? you?

HAR. Yes, I, I, I. What does all this mean?

CLE. I feel a sudden dizziness, and I must withdraw for a little while.

HAR. It will be nothing. Go quickly into the kitchen and drink a large glass of cold water, it will soon set you all right again.

SCENE VI.--HARPAGON, ELISE.

HAR. There goes one of your effeminate fops, with no more stamina than a chicken. That is what I have resolved for myself, my daughter. As to your brother, I have thought for him of a certain widow, of whom I heard this morning; and you I shall give to Mr. Anselme.

ELI. To Mr. Anselme?

HAR. Yes, a staid and prudent man, who is not above fifty, and of whose riches everybody speaks.

ELI. (). I have no wish to marry, father, if you please.

HAR. (ELISE). And I, my little girl, my darling, I wish you to marry, if you please.

ELI. (). I beg your pardon, my father.

HAR. (ELISE). I beg your pardon, my daughter.

ELI. I am the very humble servant of Mr. Anselme, but (curtseying again), with your leave, I shall not marry him.

HAR. I am your very humble servant, but (ELISE)
you will marry him this very evening.

ELI. This evening?

HAR. This evening.

ELI. (). It cannot be done, father.

HAR. (ELISE). It will be done, daughter.

ELI. No.

HAR. Yes.

ELI. No, I tell you.

HAR. Yes, I tell you.

ELI. You will never force me to do such a thing

HAR. I will force you to it.

ELI. I had rather kill myself than marry such a man.

HAR. You will not kill yourself, and you will marry him. But did you
ever see such impudence? Did ever any one hear a daughter speak in
such a fashion to her father?

ELI. But did ever anyone see a father marry his daughter after such a
fashion?

HAR. It is a match against which nothing can be said, and I am perfectly sure that everybody will approve of my choice.

ELI. And I know that it will be approved of by no reasonable person.

HAR. (VALERE). There is Valere coming. Shall we make him judge in this affair?

ELI. Willingly.

HAR. You will abide by what he says?

ELI. Yes, whatever he thinks right, I will do.

HAR. Agreed.

SCENE VII.--VALERE, HARPAGON, ELISE.

HAR. Valere, we have chosen you to decide who is in the right, my daughter or I.

VAL. It is certainly you, Sir.

HAR. But have you any idea of what we are talking about?

VAL. No; but you could not be in the wrong; you are reason itself.

HAR. I want to give her to-night, for a husband, a man as rich as he is good; and the hussy tells me to my face that she scorns to take him. What do you say to that?

VAL. What I say to it?

HAR. Yes?

VAL. Eh! eh!

HAR. What?

VAL. I say that I am, upon the whole, of your opinion, and that you cannot but be right; yet, perhaps, she is not altogether wrong;

and....

HAR. How so? Mr. Anselme is an excellent match; he is a nobleman, and a gentleman too; of simple habits, and extremely well off. He has no children left from his first marriage. Could she meet with anything more suitable?

VAL. It is true. But she might say that you are going rather fast, and that she ought to have at least a little time to consider whether her inclination could reconcile itself to....

HAR. It is an opportunity I must not allow to slip through my fingers. I find an advantage here which I should not find elsewhere, and he agrees to take her without dowry.

VAL. Without dowry?

HAR. Yes.

VAL. Ah! I have nothing more to say. A more convincing reason could not be found; and she must yield to that.

HAR. It is a considerable saving to me.

VAL. Undoubtedly; this admits of no contradiction. It is true that your daughter might represent to you that marriage is a more serious affair than people are apt to believe; that the happiness or misery of a whole life depends on it, and that an engagement which is to last till death ought not to be entered into without great consideration.

HAR. Without dowry!

VAL. That must of course decide everything. There are certainly people

who might tell you that on such occasions the wishes of a daughter are
no doubt to be considered, and that this great disparity of age, of
disposition, and of feelings might be the cause of many an unpleasant
thing in a married life.

HAR. Without dowry!

VAL. Ah! it must be granted that there is no reply to that; who in the
world could think otherwise? I do not mean to say but that there are
many fathers who would set a much higher value on the happiness of
their daughter than on the money they may have to give for their
marriage; who would not like to sacrifice them to their own interests,
and who would, above all things, try to see in a marriage that sweet
conformity of tastes which is a sure pledge of honour, tranquillity
and joy; and that....

HAR. Without dowry!

VAL. That is true; nothing more can be said. Without dowry. How can
anyone resist such arguments?

HAR. (). Ah! I fancy I hear a
dog barking. Is anyone after my money. (VALERE) Stop here,
I'll come back directly.

SCENE VIII.--ELISE, VALERE.

ELI. Surely, Valere, you are not in earnest when you speak to him in that manner?

VAL. I do it that I may not vex him, and the better to secure my ends. To resist him boldly would simply spoil everything. There are certain people who are only to be managed by indirect means, temperaments averse from all resistance, restive natures whom truth causes to rear, who always kick when we would lead them on the right road of reason, and who can only be led by a way opposed to that by which you wish them to go. Pretend to comply with his wishes; you are much more likely to succeed in the end, and....

ELI. But this marriage, Valere?

VAL. We will find some pretext for breaking it off.

ELI. But what pretext can we find if it is to be concluded to-night?

VAL. You must ask to have it delayed, and must feign some illness or other.

ELI. But he will soon discover the truth if they call in the doctor.

VAL. Not a bit of it. Do you imagine that a doctor understands what he is about? Nonsense! Don't be afraid. Believe me, you may complain of any disease you please, the doctor will be at no loss to explain to you from what it proceeds.

SCENE IX--HARPAGON, ELISE, VALERE.

HAR. (). It is nothing,
thank heaven!

VAL. (HARPAGON). In short, flight is the last
resource we have left us to avoid all this; and if your love, dear
Elise, is as strong as.... (HARPAGON) Yes, a daughter is
bound to obey her father. She has no right to inquire what a husband
offered to her is like, and when the most important question, "without
dowry," presents itself, she should accept anybody that is given her.

HAR. Good; that was beautifully said!

VAL. I beg your pardon, Sir, if I carry it a little too far, and take
upon myself to speak to her as I do.

HAR. Why, I am delighted, and I wish you to have her entirely under
your control. (ELISE) Yes, you may run away as much as you
like. I give him all the authority over you that heaven has given me,
and I will have you do all that he tells you.

VAL. After that, resist all my expostulations, if you can.

SCENE X.-HARPAGON, VALERE.

VAL. I will follow her, Sir, if you will allow me, and will continue the lecture I was giving her.

HAR. Yes, do so; you will oblige me greatly.

VAL. She ought to be kept in with a tight hand.

HAR. Quite true, you must....

VAL. Do not be afraid; I believe I shall end by convincing her.

HAR. Do so, do so. I am going to take a short stroll in the town, and I will come back again presently.

VAL. (ELISE left, and speaking as if it were to her). Yes, money is more precious than anything else in the world, and you should thank heaven that you have so worthy a man for a father. He knows what life is. When a man offers to marry a girl without a dowry, we ought to look no farther. Everything is comprised in that, and "without dowry" compensates for want of beauty, youth, birth, honour, wisdom, and probity.

HAR. Ah! the honest fellow! he speaks like an oracle. Happy is he who can secure such a servant!

ACT II.

SCENE I.--CLEANTE, LA FLECHE.

CLE. How now, you rascal! where have you been hiding? Did I not give you orders to...?

LA FL. Yes, Sir, and I came here resolved to wait for you without stirring, but your father, that most ungracious of men, drove me into the street in spite of myself, and I well nigh got a good drubbing into the bargain.

CLE. How is our affair progressing? Things are worse than ever for us, and since I left you, I have discovered that my own father is my rival.

LA FL. Your father in love?

CLE. It seems so; and I found it very difficult to hide from him what I felt at such a discovery.

LA FL. He meddling with love! What the deuce is he thinking of? Does he mean to set everybody at defiance? And is love made for people of his build?

CLE. It is to punish me for my sins that this passion has entered his head.

LA FL. But why do you hide your love from him?

CLE. That he may not suspect anything, and to make it more easy for me to fall back, if need be, upon some device to prevent this marriage. What answer did you receive?

LA FL. Indeed, Sir, those who borrow are much to be pitied, and we must put up with strange things when, like you, we are forced to pass through the hands of the usurers.

CLE. Then the affair won't come off?

LA FL. Excuse me; Mr. Simon, the broker who was recommended to us, is a very active and zealous fellow, and says he has left no stone unturned to help you. He assures me that your looks alone have won his heart.

CLE. Shall I have the fifteen thousand francs which I want?

LA FL. Yes, but under certain trifling conditions, which you must accept if you wish the bargain to be concluded.

CLE. Did you speak to the man who is to lend the money?

LA FL Oh! dear no. Things are not done in that way. He is still more anxious than you to remain unknown. These things are greater mysteries than you think. His name is not by any means to be divulged, and he is to be introduced to you to-day at a house provided by him, so that he may hear from yourself all about your position and your family; and I have not the least doubt that the mere name of your father will be sufficient to accomplish what you wish.

CLE. Particularly as my mother is dead, and they cannot deprive me of what I inherit from her.

LA FL. Well, here are some of the conditions which he has himself dictated to our go-between for you to take cognisance of, before anything is begun.

"Supposing that the lender is satisfied with all his securities, and that the borrower is of age and of a family whose property is ample, solid, secure, and free from all incumbrances, there shall be drawn up a good and correct bond before as honest a notary as it is possible to find, and who for this purpose shall be chosen by the lender, because he is the more concerned of the two that the bond should be rightly executed."

CLE. There is nothing to say against that.

LA FA. "The lender, not to burden his conscience with the least scruple, does not wish to lend his money at more than five and a half per cent."

CLE. Five and a half per cent? By Jove, that's honest! We have nothing to complain of,

LA FL. That's true.

"But as the said lender has not in hand the sum required, and as, in order to oblige the borrower, he is himself obliged to borrow from another at the rate of twenty per cent., it is but right that the said first borrower shall pay this interest, without detriment to the rest;

since it is only to oblige him that the said lender is himself forced
to borrow."

CLE. The deuce! What a Jew! what a Turk we have here! That is more
than twenty-five per cent.

LA FL. That's true; and it is the remark I made. It is for you to
consider the matter before you act.

CLE. How can I consider? I want the money, and I must therefore accept
everything.

LA FL. That is exactly what I answered.

CLE. Is there anything else?

LA FL. Only a small item.

"Of the fifteen thousand francs which are demanded, the lender will
only be able to count down twelve thousand in hard cash; instead of
the remaining three thousand, the borrower will have to take the
chattels, clothing, and jewels, contained in the following catalogue,
and which the said lender has put in all good faith at the lowest
possible figure."

CLE. What is the meaning of all that?

LA FL. I'll go through the catalogue:--

"Firstly:--A fourpost bedstead, with hangings of Hungary lace very
elegantly trimmed with olive-coloured cloth, and six chairs and a
counterpane to match; the whole in very good condition, and lined with
soft red and blue shot-silk. Item:--the tester of good pale pink

Aumale serge, with the small and the large fringes of silk."

CLE. What does he want me to do with all this?

LA FL. Wait.

"Item:--Tapestry hangings representing the loves of Gombaud and Macee. [Footnote: An old comic pastoral.] Item:--A large walnut table with twelve columns or turned legs, which draws out at both ends, and is provided beneath with six stools."

CLE. Hang it all! What am I to do with all this?

LA FL. Have patience.

"Item:--Three large matchlocks inlaid with mother-of-pearl, with rests to correspond. Item:--A brick furnace with two retorts and three receivers, very useful to those who have any taste for distilling."

CLE. You will drive me crazy.

LA FL. Gently!

"Item:--A Bologna lute with all its strings, or nearly all. Item:--A pigeon-hole table and a draught-board, and a game of mother goose, restored from the Greeks, most useful to pass the time when one has nothing to do. Item:--A lizard's skin, three feet and a half in length, stuffed with hay, a pleasing curiosity to hang on the ceiling of a room. The whole of the above-mentioned articles are really worth more than four thousand five hundred francs, and are reduced to the value of a thousand crowns through the considerateness of the lender."

CLE. Let the plague choke him with his considerateness, the wretch, the cut-throat that he is! Did ever anyone hear of such usury? Is he not satisfied with the outrageous interest he asks that he must force me to take, instead of the three thousand francs, all the old rubbish which he picks up. I shan't get two hundred crowns for all that, and yet I must bring myself to yield to all his wishes; for he is in a position to force me to accept everything, and he has me, the villain, with a knife at my throat.

LA FL. I see you, Sir, if you'll forgive my saying so, on the high-road followed by Panurge [Footnote: The real hero in Rabelais' 'Pantagruel.'] to ruin himself--taking money in advance, buying dear, selling cheap, and cutting your corn while it is still grass.

CLE. What would you have me do? It is to this that young men are reduced by the accursed avarice of their fathers; and people are astonished after that, that sons long for their death.

LA FL. No one can deny that yours would excite against his meanness the most quiet of men. I have not, thank God, any inclination gallows-ward, and among my colleagues whom I see dabbling in various doubtful affairs, I know well enough how to keep myself out of hot water, and how to keep clear of all those things which savour ever so little of the ladder; but to tell you the truth, he almost gives me, by his ways of going on, the desire of robbing him, and I should think that in doing so I was doing a meritorious action.

CLE. Give me that memorandum that I may have another look at it.

SCENE II.--HARPAGON, MR. SIMON
(CLEANTE LA FLECHE at the
back of the stage).

SIM. Yes, Sir; it is a young man who is greatly in want of money; his affairs force him to find some at any cost, and he will submit to all your conditions.

HAR. But are you sure, Mr. Simon, that there is no risk to run in this case? and do you know the name, the property, and the family of him for whom you speak?

SIM. No; I cannot tell you anything for certain, as it was by mere chance that I was made acquainted with him; but he will tell you everything himself, and his servant has assured me that you will be quite satisfied when you know who he is. All I can tell you is that his family is said to be very wealthy, that he has already lost his mother, and that he will pledge you his word, if you insist upon it, that his father will die before eight months are passed.

HAR. That is something. Charity, Mr. Simon, demands of us to gratify people whenever we have it in our power.

SIM. Evidently.

LA FL. (CLEANTE, MR. SIMON).
What does this mean? Mr. Simon talking with your father!

CLE. (LA FLECHE). Has he been told who I am, and would
you be capable of betraying me?

SIM. (CLEANTE LA FLECHE). Ah! you are in good
time! But who told you to come here? (HARPAGON) It was
certainly not I who told them your name and address; but I am of
opinion that there is no great harm done; they are people who can be
trusted, and you can come to some understanding together.

HAR. What!

SIM. (CLEANTE). This is the gentleman who wants to
borrow the fifteen thousand francs of which I have spoken to you.

HAR. What! miscreant! is it you who abandon yourself to such excesses?

CLE. What! father! is it you who stoop to such shameful deeds?

(MR. SIMON LA FLECHE .)

SCENE III.--HARPAGON, CLEANTE.

HAR. It is you who are ruining yourself by loans so greatly to be condemned!

CLE. So it is you who seek to enrich yourself by such criminal usury!

HAR. And you dare, after that, to show yourself before me?

CLE. And you dare, after that, to show yourself to the world?

HAR. Are you not ashamed, tell me, to descend to these wild excesses, to rush headlong into frightful expenses, and disgracefully to dissipate the wealth which your parents have amassed with so much toil.

CLE. Are you not ashamed of dishonouring your station by such dealings, of sacrificing honour and reputation to the insatiable desire of heaping crown upon crown, and of outdoing the most infamous devices that have ever been invented by the most notorious usurers?

HAR. Get out of my sight, you reprobate; get out of my sight!

CLE. Who is the more criminal in your opinion: he who buys the money of which he stands in need, or he who obtains, by unfair means, money for which he has no use?

HAR. Begone, I say, and do not provoke me to anger. ()
After all, I am not very much vexed at this adventure; it will be a
lesson to me to keep a better watch over all his doings.

SCENE IV.--FROSINE, HARPAGON.

FRO. Sir.

HAR. Wait a moment, I will come back and speak to you. ()
I had better go and see a little after my money.

SCENE V.--LA FLECHE, FROSINE.

LA FL. (FROSINE). The adventure is most comical.
Hidden somewhere he must have a large store of goods of all kinds, for
the list did not contain one single article which either of us
recognised.

FRO. Hallo! is it you, my poor La Fleche? How is it we meet here?

LA FL. Ah! ah! it is you, Frosine; and what have you come to do here?

FRO. What have I come to do? Why! what I do everywhere else, busy
myself about other people's affairs, make myself useful to the
community in general, and profit as much as I possibly can by the
small talent I possess. Must we not live by our wits in this world?
and what other resources have people like me but intrigue and cunning?

LA FL. Have you, then, any business with the master of this house?

FRO. Yes. I am transacting for him a certain small matter for which he
is pretty sure to give me a reward.

LA FL. He give you a reward! Ah! ah! Upon my word, you will be 'cute
if you ever get one, and I warn you that ready money is very scarce
hereabouts.

FRO. That may be, but there are certain services which wonderfully
touch our feelings.

LA FL. Your humble servant; but as yet you don't know Harpagon.
Harpagon is the human being of all human beings the least humane, the
mortal of all mortals the hardest and closest. There is no service
great enough to induce him to open his purse. If, indeed, you want
praise, esteem, kindness, and friendship, you are welcome to any
amount; but money, that's a different affair. There is nothing more
dry, more barren, than his favour and his good grace, and
"" is a word for which be has such a strong dislike that he
never says , but .

FRO. That's all very well; but I know the art of fleecing men. I have
a secret of touching their affections by flattering their hearts, and
of finding out their weak points.

LA FL. All useless here. I defy you to soften, as far as money is
concerned, the man we are speaking of. He is a Turk on that point, of
a Turkishness to drive anyone to despair, and we might starve in his
presence and never a peg would he stir. In short, he loves money
better than reputation, honour, and virtue, and the mere sight of
anyone making demands upon his purse sends him into convulsions; it is
like striking him in a vital place, it is piercing him to the heart,
it is like tearing out his very bowels! And if ... But here he comes
again; I leave you.

SCENE VI.--HARPAGON, FROSINE.

HAR. (). All is as it should be. (FROSINE) Well,
what is it, Frosine?

FRO. Bless me, how well you look! You are the very picture of health.

HAR. Who? I?

FRO. Never have I seen you looking more rosy, more hearty.

HAR. Are you in earnest?

FRO. Why! you have never been so young in your life; and I know many a
man of twenty-five who looks much older than you do.

HAR. And yet, Frosine, I have passed threescore.

FRO. Threescore! Well, and what then? You don't mean to make a trouble
of that, do you? It's the very flower of manhood, the threshold of the
prime of life.

HAR. True; but twenty years less would do me no harm, I think.

FRO. Nonsense! You've no need of that, and you are of a build to last out a hundred.

HAR. Do you really think so?

FRO. Decidedly. You have all the appearance of it. Hold yourself up a little. Ah! what a sign of long life is that line there straight between your two eyes!

HAR. You know all about that, do you?

FRO. I should think I do. Show me your hand. [Footnote: Frosine professes a knowledge of palmistry.] Dear me, what a line of life there is there!

HAR. Where?

FRO. Don't you see how far this line goes?

HAR. Well, and what does it mean?

FRO. What does it mean? There ... I said a hundred years; but no, it is one hundred and twenty I ought to have said.

HAR. Is it possible?

FRO. I tell you they will have to kill you, and you will bury your children and your children's children.

HAR. So much the better! And what news of our affair?

FRO. Is there any need to ask? Did ever anyone see me begin anything and not succeed in it? I have, especially for matchmaking, the most wonderful talent. There are no two persons in the world I could not

couple together; and I believe that, if I took it into my head, I
could make the Grand Turk marry the Republic of Venice. [Footnote: Old
enemies. The Turks took Candia from the Venetians in 1669, after a war
of twenty years.] But we had, to be sure, no such difficult thing to
achieve in this matter. As I know the ladies very well, I told them
every particular about you; and I acquainted the mother with your
intentions towards Marianne since you saw her pass in the street and
enjoy the fresh air out of her window.

HAR. What did she answer...?

FRO. She received your proposal with great joy; and when I told her
that you wished very much that her daughter should come to-night to
assist at the marriage contract which is to be signed for your own
daughter, she assented at once, and entrusted her to me for the
purpose.

HAR. You see, Frosine, I am obliged to give some supper to Mr.
Anselme, and I should like her to have a share in the feast.

FRO. You are quite right. She is to come after dinner to pay a visit
to your daughter; then she means to go from here to the fair, and
return to your house just in time for supper.

HAR. That will do very well; they shall go together in my carriage,
which I will lend them.

FRO. That will suit her perfectly.

HAR. But I say, Frosine, have you spoken to the mother about the dowry
she can give her daughter? Did you make her understand that under such
circumstances she ought to do her utmost and to make a great
sacrifice? For, after all, one does not marry a girl without her

bringing something with her.

FRO. How something! She is a girl who will bring you a clear twelve thousand francs a year?

HAR. Twelve thousand francs a year?

FRO. Yes! To begin with, she has been nursed and brought up with the strictest notions of frugality. She is a girl accustomed to live upon salad, milk, cheese, and apples, and who consequently will require neither a well served up table, nor any rich broth, nor your everlasting peeled barley; none, in short, of all those delicacies that another woman would want. This is no small matter, and may well amount to three thousand francs yearly. Besides this, she only cares for simplicity and neatness; she will have none of those splendid dresses and rich jewels, none of that sumptuous furniture in which girls like her indulge so extravagantly; and this item is worth more than four thousand francs per annum. Lastly, she has the deepest aversion to gambling; and this is not very common nowadays among women. Why, I know of one in our neighbourhood who lost at least twenty thousand francs this year. But let us reckon only a fourth of that sum. Five thousand francs a year at play and four thousand in clothes and jewels make nine thousand; and three thousand francs which we count for food, does it not make your twelve thousand francs?

HAR. Yes, that's not bad; but, after all, that calculation has nothing real in it.

FRO. Excuse me; is it nothing real to bring you in marriage a great sobriety, to inherit a great love for simplicity in dress, and the acquired property of a great hatred for gambling?

HAR. It is a farce to pretend to make up a dowry with all the expenses she will not run into. I could not give a receipt for what I do not receive; and I must decidedly get something.

FRO. Bless me! you will get enough; and they have spoken to me of a certain country where they have some property, of which you will be master.

HAR. We shall have to see to that. But, Frosine, there is one more thing that makes me uneasy. The girl is young, you know; and young people generally like those who are young like themselves, and only care for the society of the young. I am afraid that a man of my age may not exactly suit her taste, and that this may occasion in my family certain complications that would in nowise be pleasant to me.

FRO. Oh, how badly you judge her! This is one more peculiarity of which I had to speak to you. She has the greatest detestation to all young men, and only likes old people.

HAR. Does she?

FRO. I should like you to hear her talk on that subject; she cannot bear at all the sight of a young man, and nothing delights her more than to see a fine old man with a venerable beard. The oldest are to her the most charming, and I warn you beforehand not to go and make yourself any younger than you really are. She wishes for one sixty years old at least; and it is not more than six months ago that on the very eve of being married she suddenly broke off the match on learning that her lover was only fifty-six years of age, and did not put on spectacles to sign the contract.

HAR. Only for that?

FRO. Yes; she says there is no pleasure with a man of fifty-six; and she has a decided affection for those who wear spectacles.

HAR. Well, this is quite new to me.

FRO. No one can imagine how far she carries this. She has in her room a few pictures and engravings, and what do you imagine they are? An Adonis, a Cephalus, a Paris, an Apollo? Not a bit of it! Fine portraits of Saturn, of King Priam, of old Nestor, and of good father Anchises on his son's shoulders.

HAR. That's admirable. I should never have guessed such a thing; and I am very pleased to hear that she has such taste as this. Indeed had I been a woman, I should never have loved young fellows.

FRO. I should think not. Fine trumpery indeed, these young men, for any one to fall in love with. Fine jackanapes and puppies for a woman to hanker after. I should like to know what relish anyone can find in them?

HAR. Truly; I don't understand it myself, and I cannot make out how it is that some women dote so on them.

FRO. They must be downright idiots. Can any one be in his senses who thinks youth amiable? Can those curly-pated coxcombs be men, and can one really get attached to such animals?

HAR. Exactly what I say every day! With their effeminate voices, their three little bits of a beard turned up like cat's whiskers, their tow wigs, their flowing breeches and open breasts!

FRO. Yes; they are famous guys compared with yourself. In you we see something like a man. There is enough to satisfy the eye. It is thus that one should be made and dressed to inspire love.

HAR. Then you think I am pretty well?

FRO. Pretty well! I should think so; you are charming, and your face
would make a beautiful picture. Turn round a little, if you please.
You could not find anything better anywhere. Let me see you walk. You
have a well-shaped body, free and easy, as it should be, and one which
gives no sign of infirmity.

HAR. I have nothing the matter to speak of, I am thankful to say. It
is only my cough, which returns from time to time. [Footnote: Moliere
makes use even of his own infirmities. Compare act i. scene iii. This
cough killed him at last.]

FRO. That is nothing, and coughing becomes you exceedingly well.

HAR. Tell me, Frosine, has Marianne seen me yet? Has she not noticed
me when I passed by?

FRO. No; but we have had many conversations about you. I gave her an
exact description of your person, and I did not fail to make the most
of your merit, and to show her what an advantage it would be to have a
husband like you.

HAR. You did right, and I thank you very much for it.

FRO. I have, Sir, a small request to make to you. I am in danger of
losing a lawsuit for want of a little money (HARPAGON looks
grave), and you can easily help me with it, if you have pity upon
me. You cannot imagine how happy she will be to see you. (HARPAGON
.) Oh! how sure you are to please her, and how sure
that antique ruff of yours is to produce a wonderful effect on her
mind. But, above all, she will be delighted with your breeches

fastened to your doublet with tags; that will make her mad after you, and a lover who wears tags will be most welcome to her.

HAR. You send me into raptures, Frosine, by saying that.

FRO. I tell you the truth, Sir; this lawsuit is of the utmost importance for me. (HARPAGON .) If I lose it, I am for ever ruined; but a very small sum will save me. I should like you to have seen the happiness she felt when I spoke of you to her. (HARPAGON .) Joy sparkled in her eyes while I told her of all your good qualities; and I succeeded, in short, in making her look forward with the greatest impatience to the conclusion of the match.

HAR. You have given me great pleasure, Frosine, and I assure you I....

FRO. I beg of you, Sir, to grant me the little assistance I ask of you. (HARPAGON .) It will put me on my feet again, and I shall feel grateful to you for ever.

HAR. Good-bye; I must go and finish my correspondence.

FRO. I assure you, Sir, that you could not help me in a more pressing necessity.

HAR. I will see that my carriage is ready to take you to the fair.

FRO. I would not importune you so if I were not compelled by necessity.

HAR. And I will see that we have supper early, so that nobody may be ill.

FRO. Do not refuse me the service; I beg of you. You can hardly believe, Sir, the pleasure that....

HAR. I must go; somebody is calling me. We shall see each other again by and by.

FRO. (). May the fever seize you, you stingy cur, and send you to the devil and his angels! The miser has held out against all my attacks; but I must not drop the negotiation; for I have the other side, and there, at all events, I am sure of a good reward.

ACT III.

SCENE I.--HARPAGON, CLEANTE, ELISE, VALERE; DAME CLAUDE (holding a broom), MASTER JACQUES, LA MER-LUCHE, BRINDAVOINE.

HAR. Here, come here, all of you; I must give you orders for by and by, and arrange what each one will have to do. Come nearer, Dame Claude; let us begin with you. () Good;
you are ready armed, I see. To you I commit the care of cleaning up everywhere; but, above all, be very careful not to rub the furniture too hard, for fear of wearing it out. Besides this, I put the bottles under your care during supper, and if any one of them is missing, or if anything gets broken, you will be responsible for it, and pay it out of your wages.

JAC. (). A shrewd punishment that.

HAR. (DAME CLAUDE.) Now you may go.

SCENE II.--HARPAGON, CLEANTE, ELISE, VALERE, MASTER JACQUES, BRINDAVOINE, LA MERLUCHE.

HAR. To you, Brindavoine, and to you, La Merluche, belongs the duty of washing the glasses, and of giving to drink, but only when people are thirsty, and not according to the custom of certain impertinent lackeys, who urge them to drink, and put the idea into their heads when they are not thinking about it. Wait until you have been asked several times, and remember always to have plenty of water.

JAC. (). Yes; wine without water gets into one's head.

LA MER. Shall we take off our smocks, Sir?

HAR. Yes, when you see the guests coming; but be very careful not to spoil your clothes.

BRIND. You know, Sir, that one of the fronts of my doublet is covered with a large stain of oil from the lamp.

LA MER. And I, Sir, that my breeches are all torn behind, and that, saving your presence....

HAR. (LA MERLUCHE). Peace! Turn carefully towards the wall, and always face the company. (BRINDAVOINE, showing him how he is to hold his hat before his doublet, to hide the stain of oil) And you, always hold your hat in this fashion when you wait on the guests.

SCENE III.--HARPAGON; CLEANTE, ELISE, VALERE, MASTER JACQUES.

HAR. As for you, my daughter, you will look after all that is cleared off the table, and see that nothing is wasted: this care is very becoming to young girls. Meanwhile get ready to welcome my lady-love, who is coming this afternoon to pay you a visit, and will take you off to the fair with her. Do you understand what I say?

ELI. Yes, father.

SCENE IV.--HARPAGON, CLEANTE, VALERE, MASTER JACQUES.

HAR. And you, my young dandy of a son to whom I have the kindness of forgiving what happened this morning, mind you don't receive her coldly, or show her a sour face.

CLE. Receive her coldly! And why should I?

HAR. Why? why? We know pretty well the ways of children whose fathers marry again, and the looks they give to those we call stepmothers. But if you wish me to forget your last offence, I advise you, above all things, to receive her kindly, and, in short, to give her the heartiest welcome you can.

CLE. To speak the truth, father, I cannot promise you that I am very happy to see her become my stepmother; but as to receiving her properly, and as to giving her a kind welcome, I promise to obey you in that to the very letter.

HAR. Be careful you do, at least.

CLE. You will see that you have no cause to complain.

HAR. You will do wisely.

SCENE V.--HARPAGON, VALERE, MASTER JACQUES.

HAR. Valere, you will have to give me your help in this business. Now, Master Jacques, I kept you for the last.

JAC. Is it to your coachman, Sir, or to your cook you want to speak, for I am both the one and the other?

HAR. To both.

JAC. But to which of the two first?

HAR. To the cook.

JAC. Then wait a minute, if you please.

(JACQUES takes off his stable-coat and appears dressed as a cook.)

HAR. What the deuce is the meaning of this ceremony?

JAC. Now I am at your service.

HAR. I have engaged myself, Master Jacques, to give a supper to-night.

JAC. (). Wonderful!

HAR. Tell me, can you give us a good supper?

JAC. Yes, if you give me plenty of money.

HAR. The deuce! Always money! I think they have nothing else to say except money, money, money! Always that same word in their mouth, money! They always speak of money! It's their pillow companion, money!

VAL. Never did I hear such an impertinent answer! Would you call it wonderful to provide good cheer with plenty of money? Is it not the easiest thing in the world? The most stupid could do as much. But a clever man should talk of a good supper with little money.

JAC. A good supper with little money?

VAL. Yes.

JAC. (VALERE). Indeed, Mr. Steward, you will oblige me greatly by telling me your secret, and also, if you like, by filling my place as cook; for you keep on meddling here, and want to be everything.

HAR. Hold your tongue. What shall we want?

JAC. Ask that of Mr. Steward, who will give you good cheer with little money.

HAR. Do you hear? I am speaking to you, and expect you to answer me.

JAC. How many will there be at your table?

HAR. Eight or ten; but you must only reckon for eight. When there is enough for eight, there is enough for ten.

VAL. That is evident.

JAC. Very well, then; you must have four tureens of soup and five side dishes; soups, entrees....

HAR. What! do you mean to feed a whole town?

JAC. Roast....

HAR. (MASTER JACQUES'). Ah!
Wretch! you are eating up all my substance.

JAC. Entremets....

HAR. (JACQUES'). More
still?

VAL. (JACQUES). Do you mean to kill everybody? And has your master invited people in order to destroy them with over-feeding? Go and read a little the precepts of health, and ask the doctors if there is anything so hurtful to man as excess in eating.

HAR. He is perfectly right.

VAL. Know, Master Jacques, you and people like you, that a table overloaded with eatables is a real cut-throat; that, to be the true friends of those we invite, frugality should reign throughout the repast we give, and that according to the saying of one of the ancients, "We must eat to live, and not live to eat."

HAR. Ah! How well the man speaks! Come near, let me embrace you for this last saying. It is the finest sentence that I have ever heard in my life: "We must live to eat, and not eat to live." No; that isn't it. How do you say it?

VAL. That we must eat to live, and not live to eat.

HAR. (MASTER JACQUES). Yes. Do you hear that? (VALERE) Who is the great man who said that?

VAL. I do not exactly recollect his name just now.

HAR. Remember to write down those words for me. I will have them engraved in letters of gold over the mantel-piece of my dining-room.

VAL. I will not fail. As for your supper, you had better let me manage it. I will see that it is all as it should be.

HAR. Do so.

JAC. So much the better; all the less work for me.

HAR. (VALERE). We must have some of those things of which it is not possible to eat much, and that satisfy directly. Some good fat beans, and a pate well stuffed with chestnuts.

VAL. Trust to me.

HAR. Now, Master Jacques, you must clean my carriage.

JAC. Wait a moment; this is to the coachman. (JACQUES puts on his coat.) You say....

HAR. That you must clean my carriage, and have my horses ready to drive to the fair.

JAC. Your horses! Upon my word, Sir, they are not at all in a condition to stir. I won't tell you that they are laid up, for the poor things have got nothing to lie upon, and it would not be telling the truth. But you make them keep such rigid fasts that they are nothing but phantoms, ideas, and mere shadows of horses.

HAR. They are much to be pitied. They have nothing to do.

JAC. And because they have nothing to do, must they have nothing to eat? It would be much better for them, poor things, to work much and eat to correspond. It breaks my heart to see them so reduced; for, in short, I love my horses; and when I see them suffer, it seems as if it were myself. Every day I take the bread out of my own mouth to feed them; and it is being too hard-hearted, Sir, to have no compassion upon one's neighbour.

HAR. It won't be very hard work to go to the fair.

JAC. No, Sir. I haven't the heart to drive them; it would go too much against my conscience to use the whip to them in the state they are in. How could you expect them to drag a carriage? They have not even strength enough to drag themselves along.

VAL. Sir, I will ask our neighbour, Picard, to drive them; particularly as we shall want his help to get the supper ready.

JAC. Be it so. I had much rather they should die under another's hand than under mine.

VAL. Master Jacques is mightily considerate.

JAC. Mr. Steward is mightily indispensable.

HAR. Peace.

JAC. Sir, I can't bear these flatteries, and I can see that, whatever this man does, his continual watching after the bread, wine, wood, salt, and candles, is done but to curry favour and to make his court to you. I am indignant to see it all; and I am sorry to hear every day what is said of you; for, after all, I have a certain tenderness for you; and, except my horses, you are the person I like most in the world.

HAR. And I would know from you, Master Jacques, what it is that is said of me.

JAC. Yes, certainly, Sir, if I were sure you would not get angry with me.

HAR. No, no; never fear.

JAC. Excuse me, but I am sure you will be angry.

HAR. No, on the contrary, you will oblige me. I should be glad to know what people say of me.

JAC. Since you wish it, Sir, I will tell you frankly that you are the laughing-stock of everybody; that they taunt us everywhere by a thousand jokes on your account, and that nothing delights people more than to make sport of you, and to tell stories without end about your stinginess. One says that you have special almanacks printed, where

you double the ember days and vigils, so that you may profit by the
fasts to which you bind all your house; another, that you always have
a ready-made quarrel for your servants at Christmas time or when they
leave you, so that you may give them nothing. One tells a story how
not long since you prosecuted a neighbour's cat because it had eaten
up the remainder of a leg of mutton; another says that one night you
were caught stealing your horses' oats, and that your coachman,--that
is the man who was before me,--gave you, in the dark, a good sound
drubbing, of which you said nothing. In short, what is the use of
going on? We can go nowhere but we are sure to hear you pulled to
pieces. You are the butt and jest and byword of everybody; and never
does anyone mention you but under the names of miser, stingy, mean,
niggardly fellow and usurer.

HAR. (JACQUES). You are a fool, a rascal, a scoundrel,
and an impertinent wretch.

JAC. There, there! Did not I know how it would be? You would not
believe me. I told you I should make you angry if I spoke the truth?

HAR. Learn how to speak.

SCENE VI.--VALERE, MASTER JACQUES.

VAL. (). Well, Master Jacques, your frankness is badly
rewarded, I fear.

JAC. S'death! Mr. Upstart, you who assume the man of consequence, it
is no business of yours as far as I can see. Laugh at your own
cudgelling when you get it, and don't come here and laugh at mine.

VAL. Ah! Master Jacques, don't get into a passion, I beg of you.

JAC. (). He is drawing in his horns. I will put on a bold
face, and if he is fool enough to be afraid of me, I will pay him back
somewhat. (VALERE) Do you know, Mr. Grinner, that I am not
exactly in a laughing humour, and that if you provoke me too much, I
shall make you laugh after another fashion. (JACQUES
VALERE .)

VAL. Gently, gently.

JAC. How gently? And if it does not please me to go gently?

VAL. Come, come! What are you about?

JAC. You are an impudent rascal.

VAL. Master Jacques....

JAC. None of your Master Jacques here! If I take up a stick, I shall
soon make you feel it.

VAL. What do you mean by a stick? (JACQUES in
his turn.)

JAC. No; I don't say anything about that.

VAL. Do you know, Mr. Conceit, that I am a man to give you a drubbing
in good earnest?

JAC. I have no doubt of it.

VAL. That, after all, you are nothing but a scrub of a cook?

JAC. I know it very well.

VAL. And that you don't know me yet?

JAC. I beg your pardon.

VAL. You will beat me, you say?

JAC. I only spoke in jest.

VAL. I don't like your jesting, and (JACQUES) remember
that you are but a sorry hand at it.

JAC. (). Plague take all sincerity; it is a bad trade. I
give it up for the future, and will cease to tell the truth. It is all

very well for my master to beat me; but as for that Mr. Steward, what right has he to do it? I will be revenged on him if I can.

SCENE VII.--MARIANNE, FROSINE, MASTER JACQUES.

FRO. Do you know if your master is at home?

JAC. Yes, he is indeed; I know it but too well.

FRO. Tell him, please, that we are here.

SCENE VIII.--MARIANNE, FROSINE.

MAR. Ah! Frosine, how strange I feel, and how I dread this interview!

FRO. Why should you? What can you possibly dread?

MAR. Alas! can you ask me? Can you not understand the alarms of a person about to see the instrument of torture to which she is to be tied.

FRO. I see very well that to die agreeably, Harpagon is not the torture you would embrace; and I can judge by your looks that the fair young man you spoke of to me is still in your thoughts.

MAR. Yes, Frosine; it is a thing I do not wish to deny. The respectful visits he has paid at our house have left, I confess, a great impression on my heart.

FRO. But do you know who he is?

MAR. No, I do not. All I know is that he is made to be loved; that if things were left to my choice, I would much rather marry him than any other, and that he adds not a little to the horrible dread that I have of the husband they want to force upon me.

FRO. Oh yes! All those dandies are very pleasant, and can talk agreeably enough, but most of them are as poor as church mice; and it is much better for you to marry an old husband, who gives you plenty of money. I fully acknowledge that the senses somewhat clash with the end I propose, and that there are certain little inconveniences to be endured with such a husband; but all that won't last; and his death, believe me, will soon put you in a position to take a more pleasant husband, who will make amends for all.

MAR. Oh, Frosine! What a strange state of things that, in order to be happy, we must look forward to the death of another. Yet death will not fall in with all the projects we make.

FRO. You are joking. You marry him with the express understanding that he will soon leave you a widow; it must be one of the articles of the marriage contract. It would be very wrong in him not to die before three months are over. Here he is himself.

MAR. Ah! dear Frosine, what a face!

SCENE IX.--HARPAGON, MARIANNE, FROSINE.

HAR. (MARIANNE). Do not be offended, fair one, if I come to
you with my glasses on. I know that your beauty is great enough to be
seen with the naked eye; but, still, it is with glasses that we look
at the stars, and I maintain and uphold that you are a star, the most
beautiful and in the land of stars. Frosine, she does not answer,
star, it seems to me, shows no joy at the sight of me.

FRO. It is because she is still quite awe-struck, and young girls are
always shy at first, and afraid of showing what they feel.

HAR. (FROSINE). You are right. (MARIANNE) My
pretty darling, there is my daughter coming to welcome you.

SCENE X.--HARPAGON, ELISE, MARIANNE, FROSINE.

MAR. I am very late in acquitting myself of the visit I owed you.

ELI. You have done what I ought to have done. It was for me to have come and seen you first.

HAR. You see what a great girl she is; but ill weeds grow apace.

MAR. (FROSINE). Oh, what an unpleasant man!

HAR. (FROSINE). What does my fair one say?

FRO. That she thinks you perfect.

HAR. You do me too much honour, my adorable darling.

MAR. (). What a dreadful creature!

HAR. I really feel too grateful to you for these sentiments.

MAR. (). I can bear it no longer.

SCENE XI.--HARPAGON, MARIANNE, ELISE, CLEANTE, VALERE, FROSINE, BRINDAVOINE.

HAR. Here is my son, who also comes to pay his respects to you.

MAR. (FROSINE). Oh, Frosine! what a strange meeting!
He is the very one of whom I spoke to you.

FRO. (MARIANNE). Well, that is extraordinary.

HAR. You are surprised to see that my children can be so old; but I
shall soon get rid of both of them.

CLE. (MARIANNE). Madam, to tell you the truth, I little
expected such an event; and my father surprised me not a little when
he told me to-day of the decision he had come to.

MAR. I can say the same thing. It is an unexpected meeting; and I
certainly was far from being prepared for such an event.

CLE. Madam, my father cannot make a better choice, and it is a great
joy to me to have the honour of welcoming you here. At the same time,
I cannot say that I should rejoice if it were your intention to become
my stepmother. I must confess that I should find it difficult to pay
you the compliment; and it is a title, forgive me, that I cannot wish

you to have. To some this speech would seem coarse, but I feel that
you understand it. This marriage, Madam, is altogether repugnant to
me. You are not ignorant, now that you know who I am, how opposed it
is to all my own interests, and with my father's permission I hope you
will allow me to say that, if things depended on me, it would never
take place.

HAR. (). What a very impertinent speech to make; and what
a confession to make to her!

MAR. And as my answer, I must tell you that things are much the same
with me, and that, if you have any repugnance in seeing me your
stepmother, I shall have no less in seeing you my stepson. Do not
believe, I beg of you, that it is of my own will that this trouble has
come upon you. I should be deeply grieved to cause you the least
sorrow, and unless I am forced to it by a power I must obey, I give
you my word that, I will never consent to a marriage which is so
painful to you.

HAR. She is right. A foolish speech deserves a foolish answer. I beg
your pardon, my love, for the impertinence of my son. He is a silly
young fellow, who has not yet learnt the value of his own words.

MAR. I assure you that he has not at all offended me. I am thankful,
on the contrary, that he has spoken so openly. I care greatly for such
a confession from him, and if he had spoken differently, I should feel
much less esteem for him.

HAR. It is very kind of you to excuse him thus. Time will make him
wiser, and you will see that his feelings will change.

CLE. No, father, they will never change; and I earnestly beg of you,
Madam, to believe me.

HAR. Did ever anybody see such folly? He is becoming worse and worse.

CLE. Would you have me false to my inmost feelings?

HAR. Again! Change your manners, if you please.

CLE. Very well, since you wish me to speak differently. Allow me, Madam, to take for a moment my father's place; and forgive me if I tell you that I never saw in the world anybody more charming than you are; that I can understand no happiness to equal that of pleasing you, and that to be your husband is a glory, a felicity, I should prefer to the destinies of the greatest princes upon earth. Yes, Madam, to possess you is, in my mind, to possess the best of all treasures; to obtain you is all my ambition. There is nothing I would not do for so precious a conquest, and the most powerful obstacles....

HAR. Gently, gently, my son, if you please.

CLE. These are complimentary words which I speak to her in your name.

HAR. Bless me! I have a tongue of my own to explain my feelings, and I really don't care for such an advocate as you... Here, bring us some chairs.

FRO. No; I think it is better for us to go at once to the fair, in order to be back earlier, and have plenty of time for talking.

HAR. (BRINDAVOINE). Have the carriage ready at once.

SCENE XII.--HARPAGON, MARIANNE, ELISE, CLEANTE, VALERE, FROSINE.

HAR. (MARIANNE). I hope you will excuse me, my dear, but I forgot to order some refreshments for you, before you went out.

CLE. I have thought of it, father, and have ordered to be brought in here some baskets of China oranges, sweet citrons, and preserves, which I sent for in your name.

HAR. (VALERE). Valere!

VAL. (HARPAGON). He has lost his senses!

CLE. You are afraid, father, that it will not be enough? I hope, Madam, that you will have the kindness to excuse it.

MAR. It was by no means necessary.

CLE. Did you ever see, Madam, a more brilliant diamond than the one my father has upon his finger?

MAR. It certainly sparkles very much.

CLE. (). You must see

it near.

MAR. It is a beautiful one; it possesses great lustre.

CLE. (MARIANNE,).
No, Madam, it is in hands too beautiful; it is a present my father
gives you.

HAR. I?

CLE. Is it not true, father, that you wish her to keep it for your
sake?

HAR. (). What?

CLE. (MARIANNE). A strange question indeed! He is making me
signs that I am to force you to accept it.

MAR. I would not....

CLE. (MARIANNE). I beg of you.... He would not take it back.

HAR. (). I am bursting with rage!

MAR. It would be....

CLE. (MARIANNE). No; I
tell you, you will offend him.

MAR. Pray....

CLE. By no means.

HAR. (). Plague take....

CLE. He is perfectly shocked at your refusal.

HAR. (). Ah! traitor!

CLE. (MARIANNE). You see he is in despair.

HAR. (). You villain!

CLE. Really, father, it is not my fault. I do all I can to persuade her to accept it; but she is obstinate.

HAR. (). Rascal!

CLE. You are the cause, Madam, of my father scolding me.

HAR. (). Scoundrel!

CLE. (MARIANNE). You will make him ill; for goodness' sake, hesitate no longer.

FRO. (MARIANNE). Why so much ceremony? Keep the ring, since the gentleman wishes you to.

MAR. (HARPAGON). I will keep it now, Sir, in order not to make you angry, and I shall take another opportunity of returning it to you.

SCENE XIII.--HARPAGON, MARIANNE, ELISE, VALERE, FROSINE, BRINDAVOINE.

BRIND. Sir, there is a gentleman here who wants to speak to you.

HAR. Tell him that I am engaged, and that I cannot see him to-day.

BRIND. He says he has some money for you.

HAR. (MARIANNE). Pray, excuse me; I will come back directly.

SCENE XIV.--HARPAGON, MARIANNE, ELISE, CLEANTE, FROSINE, LA MERLUCHE.

LA MER. (HARPAGON).
Sir....

HAR. Oh! he has killed me.

CLE. What's the matter, father? Have you hurt yourself?

HAR. The wretch must have been bribed by some of my debtors to break my neck.

VAL. (HARPAGON). There is nothing serious.

LA MER. (HARPAGON). I beg your pardon, Sir; I thought I had better run fast to tell you....

HAR. What?

LA MER. That your two horses have lost their shoes.

HAR. Take them quickly to the smith.

CLE. In the meantime, father, I will do the honours of the house for you, and take this lady into the garden, where lunch will be brought.

SCENE XV.--HARPAGON, VALERE.

HAR. Valere, look after all this; and take care, I beseech you, to save as much of it as you can, so that we may send it back to the tradesman again.

VAL. I will.

HAR. (). Miscreant! do you mean to ruin me?

ACT IV.

SCENE I.--CLEANTE, MARIANNE, ELISE, FROSINE.

CLE. Let us come in here; we shall be much better. There is no one about us that we need be afraid of, and we can speak openly.

ELI. Yes, Madam, my brother has told me of the love he has for you. I know what sorrow and anxiety such trials as these may cause, and I assure you that I have the greatest sympathy for you.

MAR. I feel it a great comfort in my trouble to have the sympathy of a person like you, and I entreat you, Madam, ever to retain for me a friendship so capable of softening the cruelty of my fate.

FRO. You really are both very unfortunate not to have told me of all this before. I might certainly have warded off the blow, and not have carried things so far.

CLE. What could I do? It is my evil destiny which has willed it so. But you, fair Marianne, what have you resolved to do? What resolution have you taken?

MAR. Alas! Is it in my power to take any resolution? And, dependent as

I am, can I do anything else except form wishes?

CLE. No other support for me in your heart? Nothing but mere wishes? No pitying energy? No kindly relief? No active affection?

MAR. What am I to say to you? Put yourself in my place, and judge what I can possibly do. Advise me, dispose of me, I trust myself entirely to you, for I am sure that you will never ask of me anything but what is modest and seemly.

CLE. Alas! to what do you reduce me when you wish me to be guided entirely by feelings of strict duty and of scrupulous propriety.

MAR. But what would you have me do? Even if I were, for you, to divest myself of the many scruples which our sex imposes on us, I have too much regard for my mother, who has brought me up with great tenderness, for me to give her any cause of sorrow. Do all you can with her. Strive to win her. I give you leave to say and do all you wish; and if anything depends upon her knowing the true state of my feelings, by all means tell her what they are; indeed I will do it myself if necessary.

CLE. Frosine, dear Frosine, will you not help us?

FRO. Indeed, I should like to do so, as you know. I am not naturally unkind. Heaven has not given me a heart of flint, and I feel but too ready to help when I see young people loving each other in all earnestness and honesty. What can we do in this case?

CLE. Try and think a little.

MAR. Advise us.

ELI. Invent something to undo what you have done.

FRO. Rather a difficult piece of business. (MARIANNE) As far
as your mother is concerned, she is not altogether unreasonable and we
might succeed in making her give to the son the gift she reserved for
the father. (CLEANTE) But the most disheartening part of it
all is that your father is your father.

CLE. Yes, so it is.

FRO. I mean that he will bear malice if he sees that he is refused,
and he will be in no way disposed afterwards to give his consent to
your marriage. It would be well if the refusal could be made to come
from him, and you ought to try by some means or other to make him
dislike you, Marianne.

CLE. You are quite right.

FRO. Yes, right enough, no doubt. That is what ought to be done; but
how in the world are we to set about it? Wait a moment. Suppose we had
a somewhat elderly woman with a little of the ability which I possess,
and able sufficiently well to represent a lady of rank, by means of a
retinue made up in haste, and of some whimsical title of a marchioness
or viscountess, whom we would suppose to come from Lower Brittany. I
should have enough power over your father to persuade him that she is
a rich woman, in possession, besides her houses, of a hundred thousand
crowns in ready money; that she is deeply in love with him, and that
she would marry him at any cost, were she even to give him all her
money by the marriage contract. I have no doubt he would listen to the
proposal. For certainly he loves you very much, my dear, but he loves
money still better. When once he has consented to your marriage, it
does not signify much how he finds out the true state of affairs about
our marchioness.

CLE. All that is very well made up.

FRO. Leave it to me; I just remember one of my friends who will do beautifully.

CLE. Depend on my gratitude, Frosine, if you succeed. But, dear Marianne, let us begin, I beg of you, by gaining over your mother; it would be a great deal accomplished if this marriage were once broken off. Make use, I beseech you, of all the power that her tenderness for you gives you over her. Display without hesitation those eloquent graces, those all-powerful charms, with which Heaven has endowed your eyes and lips; forget not, I beseech you, those sweet persuasions, those tender entreaties, those loving caresses to which, I feel, nothing could be refused.

MAR. I will do all I can, and will forget nothing.

SCENE II.--HARPAGON, MARIANNE, ELISE, FROSINE.

HAR. (aside, and without being seen). Ah! ah! my son is kissing the hand of his intended stepmother, and his intended stepmother does not seem much averse to it! Can there be any mystery in all this?

ELI. Here comes my father.

HAR. The carriage is quite ready, and you can start when you like.

CLE. Since you are not going, father, allow me to take care of them.

HAR. No, stop here; they can easily take care of themselves, and I want you.

SCENE III.--HARPAGON, CLEANTE.

HAR. Well, now, all consideration of stepmother aside, tell me what do you think of this lady?

CLE. What I think of her?

HAR. Yes, what do you think of her appearance, her figure, her beauty and intelligence?

CLE. So, so.

HAR. But still?

CLE. To tell you the truth, I did not find her such as I expected. Her manner is that of a thorough coquette, her figure is rather awkward, her beauty very middling, and her intelligence of the meanest order. Do not suppose that I say this to make you dislike her; for if I must have a stepmother, I like the idea of this one as well as of any other.

HAR. You spoke to her just now, nevertheless....

CLE. I paid her several compliments in your name, but it was to please you.

HAR. So then you don't care for her?

CLE. Who? I? Not in the least.

HAR. I am sorry for it, for that puts an end to a scheme which had occurred to me. Since I have seen her here, I have been thinking of my own age; and I feel that people would find fault with me for marrying so young a girl. This consideration had made me determine to abandon the project, and as I had demanded her in marriage, and had given her my promise, I would have given her to you if it were not for the dislike you have for her.

CLE. To me?

HAR. To you.

CLE. In marriage?

HAR. In marriage.

CLE. It is true she is not at all to my taste; but, to please you, father, I will bring myself to marry her, if you please.

HAR. If I please! I am more reasonable than you think. I don't wish to compel you.

CLE. Excuse me! I will make an attempt to love her.

HAR. No, no; a marriage cannot be happy where there is no love.

CLE. That, my father, will, perhaps, come by and by, and it is said that love is often the fruit of marriage.

HAR. No, it is not right to risk it on the side of the man, and there are some troublesome things I don't care to run the chance of. If you had felt any inclination for her, you should have married her instead of me, but as it is, I will return to my first intention and marry her myself.

CLE. Well, father, since things are so, I had better be frank with you, and reveal our secret to you. The truth is that I have loved her ever since I saw her one day on the promenade. I intended to ask you today to let me marry her, and I was only deterred from it because you spoke of marrying her, and because I feared to displease you.

HAR. Have you ever paid her any visits?

CLE. Yes, father.

HAR. Many?

CLE. Yes; considering how long we have been acquainted.

HAR. You were well received.

CLE. Very well, but without her knowing who I was; and that is why Marianne was so surprised when she saw me today.

HAR. Have you told her of your love, and of your intention of marrying her?

CLE. Certainly, and I also spoke a little to the mother on the subject.

HAR. Did she kindly receive your proposal for her daughter?

CLE. Yes, very kindly.

HAR. And does the daughter return your love?

CLE. If I can believe appearances, she is certainly well disposed towards me.

HAR. (). Well! I am very glad to have found out this
secret; it is the very thing I wanted to know. ()
Now, look here, my son, I tell you what. You will have, if you please, to get rid of your love for Marianne, to cease to pay your attentions to a person I intend for myself, and to marry very soon the wife I have chosen for you.

CLE. So, father, it is thus you deceive me! Very well, since things are come to such a pass, I openly declare to you that I shall not give up my love for Marianne. No! understand that henceforth there is nothing from which I shall shrink in order to dispute her with you; and if you have on your side the consent of the mother, perhaps I shall have some other resources left to aid me.

HAR. What, rascal! You dare to trespass on my grounds?

CLE. It is you who trespass on mine. I was the first.

HAR. Am I not your father, and do you not owe me respect?

CLE. There are things in which children are not called upon to pay deference to their fathers; and love is no respector of persons.

HAR. My stick will make you know me better.

CLE. All your threatenings are nothing to me.

HAR. You will give up Marianne?

CLE. Never!

HAR. Bring me my stick. Quick, I say! my stick!

SCENE IV.--HARPAGON, CLEANTE, MASTER JACQUES.

JAC. Hold! hold! Gentlemen, what does this mean? What are you thinking of?

CLE. I don't care a bit for it.

JAC. (CLEANTE). Ah! Sir, gently.

HAR. He dares to speak to me with such impudence as that!

JAC. (HARPAGON). Ah! Sir, I beg of you.

CLE. I shall keep to it.

JAC, (CLEANTE). What! to your father?

HAR. Let me do it.

JAC. (HARPAGON). What! to your son? To me it's different.

HAR. I will make you judge between us, Master Jacques, so that you may see that I have right on my side.

JAC. Willingly. (CLEANTE) Go a little farther back.

HAR. There is a young girl I love and want to marry, and the scoundrel has the impudence to love her also, and wants to marry her in spite of me.

JAC. Oh! he is wrong.

HAR. Is it not an abominable thing to see a son who does not shrink from becoming the rival of his father? And is it not his bounden duty to refrain from interfering with my love?

JAC. You are quite right; stop here, and let me go and speak to him.

CLE. (MASTER JACQUES,). Very well;
if he wants to make you a judge between us, I have no objection. I care little who it is, and I don't mind referring our quarrel to you.

JAC. You do me great honour.

CLE. I am in love with a young girl who returns my affection, and who receives kindly the offer of my heart; but my father takes it into his head to disturb our love by asking her in marriage.

JAC. He certainly is wrong.

CLE. Is it not shameful for a man of his age to think of marrying? I ask you if it is right for him to fall in love? and ought he not now to leave that to younger men?

JAC. You are quite right; he is not serious; let me speak a word or two to him. (HARPAGON) Really, your son is not so extravagant as you think, and is amenable to reason. He says that he is conscious of the respect he owes you, and that he only got angry in the heat of the moment. He will willingly submit to all you wish if you will only promise to treat him more kindly than you do, and will give him in marriage a person to his taste.

HAR. Ah! tell him, Master Jacques, that he will obtain everything from me on those terms, and that, except Marianne, I leave him free to choose for his wife whomsoever he pleases.

JAC. Leave that to me. (CLEANTE) Really, your father is not so unreasonable as you make him out to me; and he tells me that it is your violence which irritated him. He only objects to your way of doing things, and is quite ready to grant you all you want, provided you will use gentle means and will give him the deference, respect, and submission that a son owes to his father.

CLE. Ah! Master Jacques, you can assure him that if he grants me Marianne, he will always find me the most submissive of men, and that I shall never do anything contrary to his pleasure.

JAC. (HARPAGON). It's all right; he consents to what you say.

HARP. Nothing could be better.

JAC. (CLEANTE). It's all settled; he is satisfied with your promises. CLE. Heaven be praised!

JAC. Gentlemen, you have nothing to do but to talk quietly over the matter together; you are agreed now, and yet you were on the point of quarrelling through want of understanding each other.

CLE. My poor Jacques, I shall be obliged to you all my life.

JAC. Don't mention it, Sir.

HAR. You have given me great pleasure, Master Jacques, and deserve a reward. (HARPAGON , JACQUES holds out his hand, butonly pulls out his handkerchief, and says ,) Go; I will remember it, I promise you.

JAC. I thank you kindly, Sir.

SCENE V.--HARPAGON, CLEANTE.

CLE. I beg your pardon, father, for having been angry.

HAR. It is nothing.

CLE. I assure you that I feel very sorry about it.

HAR. I am very happy to see you reasonable again.

CLE. How very kind of you so soon to forget my fault.

HAR. One easily forgets the faults of children when they return to their duty.

CLE. What! you are not angry with me for my extravagant behaviour?

HAR. By your submission and respectful conduct you compel me to forget my anger.

CLE. I assure you, father, I shall for ever keep in heart the remembrance of all your kindness.

HAR. And I promise you that, in future, you will obtain all you like from me.

CLE. Oh, father! I ask nothing more; it is sufficient for me that you give me Marianne.

HAR. What?

CLE. I say, father, that I am only too thankful already for what you have done, and that when you give me Marianne, you give me everything.

HAR. Who talks of giving you Marianne?

CLE. You, father.

HAR. I?

CLE. Yes.

HAR. What! is it not you who promised to give her up?

CLE. I! give her up?

HAR. Yes.

CLE. Certainly not.

HAR. Did you not give up all pretensions to her?

CLE. On the contrary, I am more determined than ever to have her.

HAR. What, scoundrel! again?

CLE. Nothing can make me change my mind.

HAR. Let me get at you again, wretch!

CLE. You can do as you please.

HAR. I forbid you ever to come within my sight.

CLE. As you like.

HAR. I abandon you.

CLE. Abandon me.

HAR. I disown you.

CLE. Disown me.

HAR. I disinherit you.

CLE. As you will.

HAR. I give you my curse.

CLE. I want none of your gifts.

SCENE VI. CLEANTE, LA FLECHE.

LA FL. (). Ah! Sir, you are
just in the nick of time. Quick! follow me.

CLE. What is the matter?

LA FL. Follow me, I say. We are saved.

CLE. How?

LA FL. Here is all you want.

CLE. What?

LA FL. I have watched for this all day.

CLE. What is it?

LA FL. Your father's treasure that I have got hold of.

CLE. How did you manage it?

LA FL. I will tell you all about it. Let us be off. I can hear him
calling out.

SCENE VII.--HARPAGON,

from the garden, rushing in without his hat,
and crying--

Thieves! thieves! assassins! murder! Justice, just heavens! I am
undone; I am murdered; they have cut my throat; they have stolen my
money! Who can it be? What has become of him? Where is he? Where is he
hiding himself? What shall I do to find him? Where shall I run? Where
shall I not run? Is he not here? Who is this? Stop! (To himself,
taking hold of his own arm) Give me back my money, wretch....
Ah...! it is myself.... My mind is wandering, and I know not where I
am, who I am, and what I am doing. Alas! my poor money! my poor money!
my dearest friend, they have bereaved me of thee; and since thou art
gone, I have lost my support, my consolation, and my joy. All is ended
for me, and I have nothing more to do in the world! Without thee it is
impossible for me to live. It is all over with me; I can bear it no
longer. I am dying; I am dead; I am buried. Is there nobody who will
call me from the dead, by restoring my dear money to me, or by telling
me who has taken it? Ah! what is it you say? It is no one. Whoever has
committed the deed must have watched carefully for his opportunity,
and must have chosen the very moment when I was talking with my
miscreant of a son. I must go. I will demand justice, and have the
whole of my house put to the torture--my maids and my valets, my son,
my daughter, and myself too. What a crowd of people are assembled
here! Everyone seems to be my thief. I see no one who does not rouse

suspicion in me. Ha! what are they speaking of there? Of him who stole my money? What noise is that up yonder? Is it my thief who is there? For pity's sake, if you know anything of my thief, I beseech you to tell me. Is he hiding there among you? They all look at me and laugh. We shall see that they all have a share in the robbery. Quick! magistrates, police, provosts, judges, racks, gibbets, and executioners. I will hang everybody, and if I do not find my money, I will hang myself afterwards.

ACT V.

SCENE I.--HARPAGON, A POLICE OFFICER.

OFF. Leave that to me. I know my business. Thank Heaven! this is not the first time I have been employed in finding out thieves; and I wish I had as many bags of a thousand francs as I have had people hanged.

HAR. Every magistrate must take this affair in hand; and if my money is not found, I shall call justice against justice itself.

OFF. We must take all needful steps. You say there was in that casket...?

HAR. Ten thousand crowns in cash.

OFF. Ten thousand crowns!

HAR. Ten thousand crowns.

OFF. A considerable theft.

HAR. There is no punishment great enough for the enormity of the crime; and if it remain unpunished, the most sacred things are no longer secure.

OFF. In what coins was that sum?

HAR. In good louis d'or and pistoles of full weight.

OFF. Whom do you suspect of this robbery?

HAR. Everybody. I wish you to take into custody the whole town and suburbs.

OFF. You must not, if you trust me, frighten anybody, but must use gentle means to collect evidence, in order afterwards to proceed with more rigour for the recovery of the sum which has been taken from you.

SCENE II.--HARPAGON, THE POLICE OFFICER, MASTER JACQUES.

JAC. (at the end of the stage, turning back to the door by which he came in). I am coming back. Have his throat cut at once; have his feet singed; put him in boiling water, and hang him up to the ceiling.

HAR. What! Him who has robbed me?

JAC. I was speaking of a sucking pig that your steward has just sent me; and I want to have it dressed for you after my own fancy.

HAR. This is no longer the question; and you have to speak of something else to this gentleman.

OFF. (JACQUES). Don't get frightened. I am not a man to cause any scandal, and matters will be carried on by gentle means.

JAC. (HARPAGON). Is this gentleman coming to supper with you?

OFF. You must, in this case, my good man, hide nothing from your master.

JAC. Indeed, Sir, I will show you all I know, and will treat you in the best manner I possibly can.

OFF. That's not the question.

JAC. If I do not give as good fare as I should like, it is the fault of your steward, who has clipped my wings with the scissors of his economy.

HAR. Rascal! We have other matters to talk about than your supper; and I want you to tell me what has become of the money which has been stolen from me.

JAC. Some money has been stolen from you?

HAR. Yes, you rascal! And I'll have you hanged if you don't give it me back again.

OFF. (HARPAGON). Pray, don't be hard upon him. I see by his looks that he is an honest fellow, and that he will tell you all you want to know without going to prison. Yes, my friend, if you confess, no harm shall come to you, and you shall be well rewarded by your master. Some money has been stolen from him, and it is not possible that you know nothing about it.

JAC. (). The very thing I wanted in order to be revenged of our steward. Ever since he came here, he has been the favourite, and his advice is the only one listened to. Moreover, I have forgotten neither the cudgelling of to-day nor....

HAR. What are you muttering about there?

OFF. (HARPAGON). Leave him alone. He is preparing himself to satisfy you; I told you that he was an honest fellow.

JAC. Sir, since you want me to tell you what I know, I believe it is your steward who has done this.

HAR. Valere?

JAC. Yes.

HAR. He who seemed so faithful to me!

JAC. Himself. I believe that it is he who has robbed you.

HAR. And what makes you believe it?

JAC. What makes me believe it?

HAR. Yes.

JAC. I believe it...because I believe it.

OFF. But you must tell us the proofs you have.

HAR. Did you see him hanging about the place where I had put my money?

JAC. Yes, indeed. Where was your money?

HAR. In the garden.

JAC. Exactly; I saw him loitering about in the garden; and in what was your money?

HAR. In a casket.

JAC. The very thing. I saw him with a casket.

HAR. And this casket, what was it like? I shall soon see if it is mine.

JAC. What it was like?

HAR. Yes.

JAC. It was like...like a casket.

OFF. Of course. But describe it a little, to see if it is the same.

JAC. It was a large casket.

HAR. The one taken from me is a small one.

JAC. Yes, small if you look at it in that way; but I call it large because of what it contains.

HAR. And what colour was it?

JAC. What colour?

OFF. Yes.

JAC. Of a colour...of a certain colour.... Can't you help me to find the word?

HAR. Ugh!

JAC. Red; isn't it?

HAR. No, grey.

JAC. Ha! yes, reddish-grey! That's what I meant.

HAR. There is no doubt about it, it's my casket for certain. Write down his evidence, Sir! Heavens! whom can we trust after that? We must never swear to anything, and I believe now that I might rob my own self.

JAC. (HARPAGON). There he is coming back, Sir; I beg of you not to go and tell him that it was I who let it all out, Sir.

SCENE III.-HARPAGON, THE POLICE OFFICER, VALERE, MASTER JACQUES.

HAR. Come, come near, and confess the most abominable action, the most horrible crime, that was ever committed.

VAL. What do you want, Sir?

HAR. What, wretch! you do not blush for shame after such a crime?

VAL. Of what crime do you speak?

HAR. Of what crime I speak? Base villain, as if you did not know what I mean! It is in vain for you to try to hide it; the thing is discovered, and I have just heard all the particulars. How could you thus abuse my kindness, introduce yourself on purpose into my house to betray me, and to play upon me such an abominable trick?

VAL. Sir, since everything is known to you, I will neither deny what I have done nor will I try to palliate it.

JAC. (). Oh! oh! Have I guessed the truth?

VAL. I intended to speak to you about it, and I was watching for a favourable opportunity; but, as this is no longer possible, I beg of you not to be angry, and to hear my motives.

HAR. And what fine motives can you possibly give me, infamous thief?

VAL. Ah! Sir, I do not deserve these names. I am guilty towards you, it is true; but, after all, my fault is pardonable.

HAR. How pardonable? A premeditated trick, and such an assassination as this!

VAL. I beseech you not to be so angry with me. When you have heard all I have to say, you will see that the harm is not so great as you make it out to be.

HAR. The harm not so great as I make it out to be! What! my heart's blood, scoundrel!

VAL. Your blood, Sir, has not fallen into bad hands. My rank is high enough not to disgrace it, and there is nothing in all this for which reparation cannot be made.

HAR. It is, indeed, my intention that you should restore what you have taken from me.

VAL. Your honour, Sir, shall be fully satisfied.

HAR. Honour is not the question in all this. But tell me what made you commit such a deed?

VAL. Alas! do you ask it?

HAR. Yes, I should rather think that I do.

VAL. A god, Sir, who carries with him his excuses for all he makes people do: Love.

HAR. Love?

VAL. Yes.

HAR. Fine love that! fine love, indeed! the love of my gold!

VAL. No, Sir, it is not your wealth that has tempted me, it is not that which has dazzled me; and I swear never to pretend to any of your possessions, provided you leave me what I have.

HAR. In the name of all the devils, no, I shall not leave it to you. But did anyone ever meet with such villainy! He wishes to keep what he has robbed me of!

VAL. Do you call that a robbery?

HAR. If I call that a robbery? A treasure like that!

VAL. I readily acknowledge that it is a treasure, and the most precious one you have. But it will not be losing it to leave it to me. I ask you on my knees to leave in my possession this treasure so full of charms; and if you do right, you will grant it to me.

HAR. I will do nothing of the kind. What in the world are you driving at?

VAL. We have pledged our faith to each other, and have taken an oath never to forsake one another.

HAR. The oath is admirable, and the promise strange enough!

VAL. Yes, we are engaged to each other for ever.

HAR. I know pretty well how to disengage you, I assure you of that.

VAL. Nothing but death can separate us.

HAR. You must be devilishly bewitched by my money.

VAL. I have told you already, Sir, that it is not self-interest which has prompted me to what I have done. It was not that which prompted my heart; a nobler motive inspired me.

HAR. We shall hear presently that it is out of Christian charity that he covets my money! But I will put a stop to all this, and justice, impudent rascal, will soon give me satisfaction.

VAL. You will do as you please, and I am ready to suffer all the violence you care to inflict upon me, but I beg of you to believe, at least, that if there is any harm done, I am the only one guilty, and that your daughter has done nothing wrong in all this.

HAR. I should think not! It would be strange, indeed, if my daughter had a share in this crime. But I will have that treasure back again, and you must confess to what place you have carried it off. [Footnote: A good deal of the mystification is lost in the translation through the necessity of occasionally putting for , and for Elise.]

VAL. I have not carried it off, and it is still in your house.

HAR. (). O my beloved casket! (VALERE) My treasure has not left my house?

VAL. No, Sir.

HAR. Well, then, tell me, have you taken any liberties with...?

VAL. Ah! Sir, you wrong us both; the flame with which I burn is too pure, too full of respect.

HAR. (). He burns for my casket!

VAL. I had rather die than show the least offensive thought: I found too much modesty and too much purity for that.

HAR. (). My cash-box modest!

VAL. All my desires were limited to the pleasures of sight, and nothing criminal has profaned the passion those fair eyes have inspired me with.

HAR. (). The fair eyes of my cash-box! He speaks of it as a lover does of his mistress.

VAL. Dame Claude knows the whole truth, and she can bear witness to it.

HAR. Hallo! my servant is an accomplice in this affair?

VAL. Yes, Sir, she was a witness to our engagement; and it was after being sure of the innocence of my love that she helped me to persuade your daughter to engage herself to me.

HAR. Ah! () Has the fear of justice made him lose his senses? (VALERE) What rubbish are you talking about my daughter?

VAL. I say, Sir, that I found it most difficult to make her modesty consent to what my love asked of her.

HAR. The modesty of whom?

VAL. Of your daughter; and it was only yesterday that she could make up her mind to sign our mutual promise of marriage.

HAR. My daughter has signed a promise of marriage?

VAL. Yes, Sir, and I have also signed.

HAR. O heavens! another misfortune!

JAC. (OFFICER). Write, Sir, write.

HAR. Aggravation of misery! Excess of despair! (OFFICER)
Sir, discharge your duty, and draw me up an indictment against him as a thief and a suborner.

JAC. As a thief and a suborner.

VAL. These are names which I do not deserve, and when you know who I am....

SCENE IV.--HARPAGON, ELISE, MARIANNE, VALERE, FROSINE, MASTER JACQUES, THE POLICE OFFICER.

HAR. Ah! guilty daughter! unworthy of a father like me! is it thus that you put into practice the lessons I have given you? You give your love to an infamous thief, and engage yourself to him without my consent! But you shall both be disappointed. (ELISE) Four strong walls will answer for your conduct in the future; (VALERE) and good gallows, impudent thief, shall do me justice for your audacity.

VAL. Your anger will be no judge in this affair, and I shall at least have a hearing before I am condemned.

HAR. I was wrong to say gallows; you shall be broken alive on the wheel.

ELI. (). Ah! my father, be more merciful, I beseech you, and do not let your paternal authority drive matters to extremes. Do not suffer yourself to be carried away by the first outburst of your anger, but give yourself time to consider what you do. Take the trouble of inquiring about him whose conduct has offended you. He is not what you imagine, and you will think it less strange that I should have given myself to him, when you know that without him you would long ago have lost me for ever. Yes, father, it is he who saved me from the great danger I ran in the waters, and to whom you owe the life of that very daughter who....

HAR. All this is nothing; and it would have been much better for me if he had suffered you to be drowned rather than do what he has done.

ELI. My father, I beseech you, in the name of paternal love, grant me....

HAR. No, no. I will hear nothing, and justice must have its course.

JAC. (). You shall pay me for the blows you gave me.

FRO. What a perplexing state of affairs!

SCENE V.--ANSELME, HARPAGON, ELISE, MARI-ANNE, FROSINE, VALERE, THE POLICE OFFICER, MASTER JACQUES.

ANS. What can have happened, Mr. Harpagon? You are quite upset.

HAR. Ah, Mr. Anselme, you see in me the most unfortunate of men; and you can never imagine what vexation and disorder is connected with the contract you have come to sign! I am attacked in my property; I am attacked in my honour; and you see there a scoundrel and a wretch who has violated the most sacred rights, who has introduced himself into my house as a servant in order to steal my money, and seduce my daughter.

VAL. Who ever thought of your money about which you rave?

HAR. Yes; they have given each other a promise of marriage. This insult concerns you, Mr. Anselme; and it is you who ought to be plaintiff against him, and who at your own expense ought to prosecute him to the utmost, in order to be revenged.

ANS. It is not my intention to force anybody to marry me, and to lay claim to a heart which has already bestowed itself; but as far as your interests are concerned, I am ready to espouse them as if they were my own.

HAR. This is the gentleman, an honest commissary, who has promised that he will omit nothing of what concerns the duties of his office. (OFFICER, VALERE) Charge him, Sir, as he ought to be, and make matters very criminal.

VAL. I do not see what crime they can make of my passion for your daughter, nor the punishment you think I ought to be condemned to for our engagement; when it is known who I am....

HAR. I don't care a pin for all those stories, and the world is full, nowadays, of those pretenders to nobility, of those impostors, who take advantage of their obscurity and deck themselves out insolently with the first illustrious name that comes into their head.

VAL. Know that I am too upright to adorn myself with a name which is not mine, and that all Naples can bear testimony to my birth!

ANS. Softly! Take care of what you are about to say. You speak before a man to whom all Naples is known, and who can soon see if your story is true.

VAL. (). I am not the man to fear anything; and if all Naples is known to you, you know who was Don Thomas d'Alburci.

ANS. Certainly; I know who he is, and few people know him better than I do.

HAR. I care neither for Don Thomas nor Don Martin. (Seeing two candles burning, he blows one out.)

ANS. Have patience and let him speak; we shall soon know what he has to say of him.

VAL. That it is to him that I owe my birth.

ANS. To him?

VAL. Yes.

ANS. Nonsense; you are laughing. Try and make out a more likely story, and don't pretend to shelter yourself under such a piece of imposture.

VAL. Consider your words better before you speak; it is no imposture, and I say nothing here that I cannot prove.

ANS. What! You dare to call yourself the son of Don Thomas d'Alburci?

VAL. Yes, I dare to do so; and I am ready to maintain the truth against anyone, who ever he may be.

ANS. This audacity is marvellous. Learn to your confusion that it is now at least sixteen years ago since the man of whom you speak died in a shipwreck at sea with his wife and children, when he was trying to save their lives from the cruel persecutions which accompanied the troubles at Naples, and which caused the banishment of several noble families. VAL. Yes; but learn to your confusion that his son, seven years of age, was, with a servant, saved from the wreck by a Spanish vessel, and that this son is he who now speaks to you. Learn that the captain of that ship, touched with compassion at my misfortune, loved me; that he had me brought up as his own son, and that the profession of arms has been my occupation ever since I was fit for it; that lately I heard that my father is not dead, as I thought he was; that, passing this way to go and find him out, an accident, arranged by heaven, brought to my sight the charming Elise; that the sight of her made me a slave to her beauty, and that the violence of my love and the harshness of her father made me take the resolution to come into his house disguised as a servant, and to send some one else to look after my parents.

ANS. But what other proofs have you besides your own words that all this is not a fable based by you upon truth.

VAL. What proofs? The captain of the Spanish vessel; a ruby seal which belonged to my father; an agate bracelet which my mother put upon my arm; and old Pedro, that servant who was saved with me from the wreck.

MAR. Alas! I can answer here for what you have said; that you do not deceive us; and all you say clearly tells me that you are my brother.

VAL. You my sister!

MAR. Yes, my heart was touched as soon as you began to speak; and our mother, who will be delighted at seeing you, often told me of the misfortunes of our family. Heaven spared us also in that dreadful wreck; but our life was spared at the cost of our liberty, for my mother and myself were taken up by pirates from the wreck of our vessel. After ten years of slavery a lucky event gave us back to liberty, and we returned to Naples, where we found all our property sold, and could hear no news of our father. We embarked for Genoa, where my mother went to gather what remained of a family estate which had been much disputed. Leaving her unjust relatives, she came here, where she has lived but a weary life.

ANS. O heaven! how wonderful are thy doings, and how true it is that it only belongs to thee to work miracles! Come to my arms, my children, and share the joy of your happy father!

VAL. You are our father?

MAR. It was for you that my mother wept?

ANS. Yes, my daughter; yes, my son; I am Don Thomas d'Alburci, whom heaven saved from the waves, with all the money he had with him, and who, after sixteen years, believing you all dead, was preparing, after long journeys, to seek the consolations of a new family in marrying a gentle and virtuous woman. The little security there was for my life in Naples has made me abandon the idea of returning there, and having found the means of selling what I had, I settled here under the name of Anselme. I wished to forget the sorrows of a name associated with so many and great troubles.

HAR. (ANSELME). He is your son?

ANS. Yes.

HAR. That being so, I make you responsible for the ten thousand crowns that he has stolen from me.

ANS. He steal anything from you!

HAR. Yes.

VAL. Who said so?

HAR. Master Jacques.

VAL. (MASTER JACQUES). You say that?

JAC. You see that I am not saying anything.

HAR. He certainly did. There is the officer who has received his deposition.

VAL. Can you really believe me capable of such a base action?

HAR. Capable or not capable, I must find my money.

SCENE VI.--HARPAGON, ANSELME, ELISE, MARIANNE, CLEANTE, VALERE, FROSINE, THE POLICE OFFICER, MASTER JACQUES, LA FLECHE.

CLE. Do not grieve for your money, father, and accuse any one. I have news of it, and I come here to tell you that if you consent to let me marry Marianne, your money will be given back to you.

HAR. Where is it?

CLE. Do not trouble yourself about that. It is in a safe place, and I answer for it; everything depends on your resolve. It is for you to decide, and you have the choice either of losing Marianne or your cash-box.

HAR. Has nothing been taken out?

CLE. Nothing at all. Is it your intention to agree to this marriage, and to join your consent to that of her mother, who leaves her at liberty to do as she likes?

MAR. (CLEANTE). But you do not know that this consent is no longer sufficient, and that heaven has given me back a brother (VALERE), at the same time that it has given me back a

father (ANSELME); and you have now to obtain me from
him.

ANS. Heaven, my dear children, has not restored you to me that I might
oppose your wishes. Mr. Harpagon, you must be aware that the choice of
a young girl is more likely to fall upon the son than upon the father.
Come, now, do not force people to say to you what is unnecessary, and
consent, as I do, to this double marriage.

HAR. In order for me to be well advised, I must see my casket.

CLE. You shall see it safe and sound.

HAR. I have no money to give my children in marriage.

ANS. Never mind, I have some; do not let this trouble you.

HAR. Do you take upon yourself to defray the expenses of these two
weddings?

ANS. Yes, I will take this responsibility upon myself. Are you
satisfied?

HAR. Yes, provided you order me a new suit of clothes for the wedding.

ANS. Agreed! Let us go and enjoy the blessings this happy day brings
us.

OFF. Stop, Sirs, stop; softly, if you please. Who is to pay me for my
writing?

HAR. We have nothing to do with your writing.

OFF. Indeed! and yet I do not pretend to have done it for nothing.

HAR. (MASTER JACQUES). There is a fellow you can hang in payment!

JAC. Alas! what is one to do? I receive a good cudgelling for telling the truth, and now they would hang me for lying.

ANS. Mr. Harpagon, you must forgive him this piece of imposture.

HAR. You will pay the officer then?

ANS. Let it be so. Let us go quickly, my children, to share our joy with your mother!

HAR. And I to see my dear casket

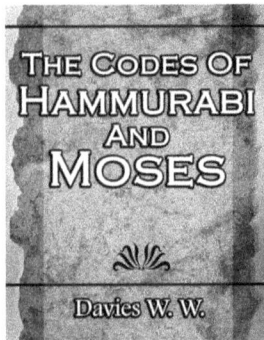

The Codes Of Hammurabi And Moses
W. W. Davies

The discovery of the Hammurabi Code is one of the greatest achievements of archaeology, and is of paramount interest, not only to the student of the Bible, but also to all those interested in ancient history...

Religion   **ISBN: *1-59462-338-4***

QTY

Pages:132
MSRP $12.95

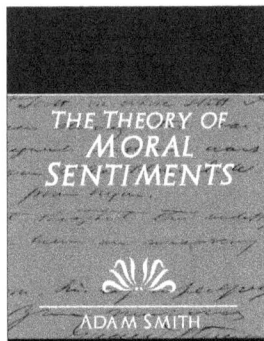

The Theory of Moral Sentiments
Adam Smith

This work from 1749. contains original theories of conscience amd moral judgment and it is the foundation for systemof morals.

Philosophy ISBN: *1-59462-777-0*

QTY

Pages:536
MSRP $19.95

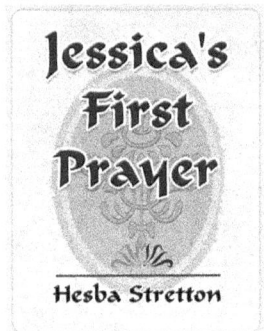

Jessica's First Prayer
Hesba Stretton

In a screened and secluded corner of one of the many railway-bridges which span the streets of London there could be seen a few years ago, from five o'clock every morning until half past eight, a tidily set-out coffee-stall, consisting of a trestle and board, upon which stood two large tin cans, with a small fire of charcoal burning under each so as to keep the coffee boiling during the early hours of the morning when the work-people were thronging into the city on their way to their daily toil...

QTY

Pages:84

Childrens   ISBN: *1-59462-373-2*   *MSRP $9.95*

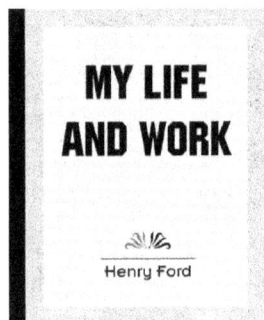

My Life and Work
Henry Ford

Henry Ford revolutionized the world with his implementation of mass production for the Model T automobile. Gain valuable business insight into his life and work with his own auto-biography... "We have only started on our development of our country we have not as yet, with all our talk of wonderful progress, done more than scratch the surface. The progress has been wonderful enough but..."

QTY

Pages:300

Biographies/   ISBN: *1-59462-198-5*   *MSRP $21.95*

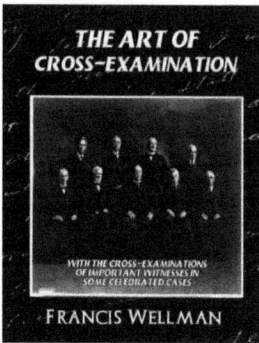

The Art of Cross-Examination
Francis Wellman

QTY

I presume it is the experience of every author, after his first book is published upon an important subject, to be almost overwhelmed with a wealth of ideas and illustrations which could readily have been included in his book, and which to his own mind, at least, seem to make a second edition inevitable. Such certainly was the case with me; and when the first edition had reached its sixth impression in five months, I rejoiced to learn that it seemed to my publishers that the book had met with a sufficiently favorable reception to justify a second and considerably enlarged edition. ..

Reference   **ISBN: *1-59462-647-2***

Pages:412

MSRP $19.95

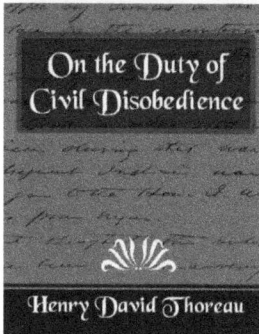

On the Duty of Civil Disobedience
Henry David Thoreau

QTY

Thoreau wrote his famous essay, On the Duty of Civil Disobedience, as a protest against an unjust but popular war and the immoral but popular institution of slave-owning. He did more than write—he declined to pay his taxes, and was hauled off to gaol in consequence. Who can say how much this refusal of his hastened the end of the war and of slavery ?

Law   **ISBN: *1-59462-747-9***

Pages:48

MSRP $7.45

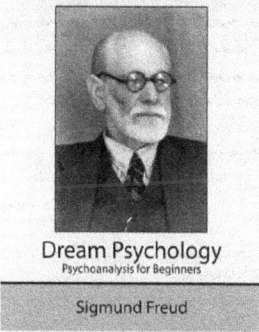

Dream Psychology Psychoanalysis for Beginners
Sigmund Freud

QTY

Sigmund Freud, born Sigismund Schlomo Freud (May 6, 1856 - September 23, 1939), was a Jewish-Austrian neurologist and psychiatrist who co-founded the psychoanalytic school of psychology. Freud is best known for his theories of the unconscious mind, especially involving the mechanism of repression; his redefinition of sexual desire as mobile and directed towards a wide variety of objects; and his therapeutic techniques, especially his understanding of transference in the therapeutic relationship and the presumed value of dreams as sources of insight into unconscious desires.

Psychology   **ISBN: *1-59462-905-6***

Pages:196

MSRP $15.45

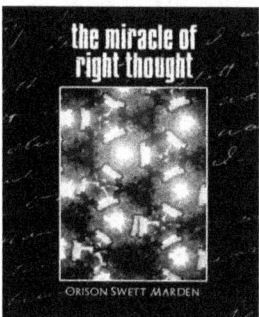

The Miracle of Right Thought
Orison Swett Marden

QTY

Believe with all of your heart that you will do what you were made to do. When the mind has once formed the habit of holding cheerful, happy, prosperous pictures, it will not be easy to form the opposite habit. It does not matter how improbable or how far away this realization may see, or how dark the prospects may be, if we visualize them as best we can, as vividly as possible, hold tenaciously to them and vigorously struggle to attain them, they will gradually become actualized, realized in the life. But a desire, a longing without endeavor, a yearning abandoned or held indifferently will vanish without realization.

Self Help   **ISBN: *1-59462-644-8***

Pages:360

MSRP $25.45

The Rosicrucian Cosmo-Conception Mystic Christianity *by Max Heindel*   ISBN: 1-59462-188-8   **$38.95**
The Rosicrucian Cosmo-conception is not dogmatic, neither does it appeal to any other authority than the reason of the student. It is: not controversial, but is: sent forth in the, hope that it may help to clear...   New Age/Religion Pages 646

Abandonment To Divine Providence *by Jean-Pierre de Caussade*   ISBN: 1-59462-228-0   **$25.95**
"The Rev. Jean Pierre de Caussade was one of the most remarkable spiritual writers of the Society of Jesus in France in the 18th Century. His death took place at Toulouse in 1751. His works have gone through many editions and have been republished...   Inspirational/Religion Pages 400

Mental Chemistry *by Charles Haanel*   ISBN: 1-59462-192-6   **$23.95**
Mental Chemistry allows the change of material conditions by combining and appropriately utilizing the power of the mind. Much like applied chemistry creates something new and unique out of careful combinations of chemicals the mastery of mental chemistry...   New Age Pages 354

The Letters of Robert Browning and Elizabeth Barret Barrett 1845-1846 vol II   ISBN: 1-59462-193-4   **$35.95**
by Robert Browning and Elizabeth Barrett   Biographies Pages 596

Gleanings In Genesis (volume I) *by Arthur W. Pink*   ISBN: 1-59462-130-6   **$27.45**
Appropriately has Genesis been termed "the seed plot of the Bible" for in it we have, in germ form, almost all of the great doctrines which are afterwards fully developed in the books of Scripture which follow...   Religion/Inspirational Pages 420

The Master Key *by L. W. de Laurence*   ISBN: 1-59462-001-6   **$30.95**
In no branch of human knowledge has there been a more lively increase of the spirit of research during the past few years than in the study of Psychology, Concentration and Mental Discipline. The requests for authentic lessons in Thought Control, Mental Discipline and...   New Age/Business Pages 422

The Lesser Key Of Solomon Goetia *by L. W. de Laurence*   ISBN: 1-59462-092-X   **$9.95**
This translation of the first book of the "Lemegton" which is now for the first time made accessible to students of Talismanic Magic was done, after careful collation and edition, from numerous Ancient Manuscripts in Hebrew, Latin, and French...   New Age/Occult Pages 92

Rubaiyat Of Omar Khayyam *by Edward Fitzgerald*   ISBN:1-59462-332-5   **$13.95**
Edward Fitzgerald, whom the world has already learned, in spite of his own efforts to remain within the shadow of anonymity, to look upon as one of the rarest poets of the century, was born at Bredfield, in Suffolk, on the 31st of March, 1809. He was the third son of John Purcell...   Music Pages 172

Ancient Law *by Henry Maine*   ISBN: 1-59462-128-4   **$29.95**
The chief object of the following pages is to indicate some of the earliest ideas of mankind, as they are reflected in Ancient Law, and to point out the relation of those ideas to modern thought.   Religion/History Pages 452

Far-Away Stories *by William J. Locke*   ISBN: 1-59462-129-2   **$19.45**
"Good wine needs no bush, but a collection of mixed vintages does. And this book is just such a collection. Some of the stories I do not want to remain buried for ever in the museum files of dead magazine-numbers an author's not unpardonable vanity..."   Fiction Pages 272

Life of David Crockett *by David Crockett*   ISBN: 1-59462-250-7   **$27.45**
"Colonel David Crockett was one of the most remarkable men of the times in which he lived. Born in humble life, but gifted with a strong will, an indomitable courage, and unremitting perseverance...   Biographies/New Age Pages 424

Lip-Reading *by Edward Nitchie*   ISBN: 1-59462-206-X   **$25.95**
Edward B. Nitchie, founder of the New York School for the Hard of Hearing, now the Nitchie School of Lip-Reading, Inc, wrote "LIP-READING Principles and Practice". The development and perfecting of this meritorious work on lip-reading was an undertaking...   How-to Pages 400

A Handbook of Suggestive Therapeutics, Applied Hypnotism, Psychic Science   ISBN: 1-59462-214-0   **$24.95**
by Henry Munro   Health/New Age/Health/Self-help Pages 376

A Doll's House: and Two Other Plays *by Henrik Ibsen*   ISBN: 1-59462-112-8   **$19.95**
Henrik Ibsen created this classic when in revolutionary 1848 Rome. Introducing some striking concepts in playwriting for the realist genre, this play has been studied the world over.   Fiction/Classics/Plays 308

The Light of Asia *by sir Edwin Arnold*   ISBN: 1-59462-204-3   **$13.95**
In this poetic masterpiece, Edwin Arnold describes the life and teachings of Buddha. The man who was to become known as Buddha to the world was born as Prince Gautama of India but he rejected the worldly riches and abandoned the reigns of power when...   Religion/History/Biographies Pages 170

The Complete Works of Guy de Maupassant *by Guy de Maupassant*   ISBN: 1-59462-157-8   **$16.95**
"For days and days, nights and nights, I had dreamed of that first kiss which was to consecrate our engagement, and I knew not on what spot I should put my lips..."   Fiction/Classics Pages 240

The Art of Cross-Examination *by Francis L. Wellman*   ISBN: 1-59462-309-0   **$26.95**
Written by a renowned trial lawyer, Wellman imparts his experience and uses case studies to explain how to use psychology to extract desired information through questioning.   How-to/Science/Reference Pages 408

Answered or Unanswered? *by Louisa Vaughan*   ISBN: 1-59462-248-5   **$10.95**
Miracles of Faith in China   Religion Pages 112

The Edinburgh Lectures on Mental Science (1909) *by Thomas*   ISBN: 1-59462-008-3   **$11.95**
This book contains the substance of a course of lectures recently given by the writer in the Queen Street Hail, Edinburgh. Its purpose is to indicate the Natural Principles governing the relation between Mental Action and Material Conditions...   New Age/Psychology Pages 148

Ayesha *by H. Rider Haggard*   ISBN: 1-59462-301-5   **$24.95**
Verily and indeed it is the unexpected that happens! Probably if there was one person upon the earth from whom the Editor of this, and of a certain previous history, did not expect to hear again...   Classics Pages 380

Ayala's Angel *by Anthony Trollope*   ISBN: 1-59462-352-X   **$29.95**
The two girls were both pretty, but Lucy who was twenty-one who supposed to be simple and comparatively unattractive, whereas Ayala was credited, as her Bombwhat romantic name might show, with poetic charm and a taste for romance. Ayala when her father died was nineteen...   Fiction Pages 484

The American Commonwealth *by James Bryce*   ISBN: 1-59462-286-8   **$34.45**
An interpretation of American democratic political theory. It examines political mechanics and society from the perspective of Scotsman James Bryce   Politics Pages 572

Stories of the Pilgrims *by Margaret P. Pumphrey*   ISBN: 1-59462-116-0   **$17.95**
This book explores pilgrims religious oppression in England as well as their escape to Holland and eventual crossing to America on the Mayflower, and their early days in New England...   History Pages 268

www.bookjungle.com *email: sales@bookjungle.com fax: 630-214-0564 mail: Book Jungle PO Box 2226 Champaign, IL 61825*

QTY

The Fasting Cure *by Sinclair Upton*   ISBN: *1-59462-222-1* **$13.95**
In the Cosmopolitan Magazine for May, 1910, and in the Contemporary Review (London) for April, 1910, I published an article dealing with my experiences in fasting. I have written a great many magazine articles, but never one which attracted so much attention... New Age/Self Help/Health Pages 164

Hebrew Astrology *by Sepharial*   ISBN: *1-59462-308-2* **$13.45**
In these days of advanced thinking it is a matter of common observation that we have left many of the old landmarks behind and that we are now pressing forward to greater heights and to a wider horizon than that which represented the mind-content of our progenitors...   Astrology Pages 144

Thought Vibration or The Law of Attraction in the Thought World   ISBN: *1-59462-127-6* **$12.95**
by William Walker Atkinson   *Psychology/Religion Pages 144*

Optimism *by Helen Keller*   ISBN: *1-59462-108-X* **$15.95**
Helen Keller was blind, deaf, and mute since 19 months old, yet famously learned how to overcome these handicaps, communicate with the world, and spread her lectures promoting optimism. An inspiring read for everyone...   Biographies/Inspirational Pages 84

Sara Crewe *by Frances Burnett*   ISBN: *1-59462-360-0* **$9.45**
In the first place, Miss Minchin lived in London. Her home was a large, dull, tall one, in a large, dull square, where all the houses were alike, and all the sparrows were alike, and where all the door-knockers made the same heavy sound...   Childrens/Classic Pages 88

The Autobiography of Benjamin Franklin *by Benjamin Franklin*   ISBN: *1-59462-135-7* **$24.95**
The Autobiography of Benjamin Franklin has probably been more extensively read than any other American historical work, and no other book of its kind has had such ups and downs of fortune. Franklin lived for many years in England, where he was agent...   Biographies/History Pages 332

Name	
Email	
Telephone	
Address	
City, State ZIP	

☐ Credit Card   ☐ Check / Money Order

Credit Card Number	
Expiration Date	
Signature	

Please Mail to: Book Jungle
PO Box 2226
Champaign, IL 61825
or Fax to: 630-214-0564

ORDERING INFORMATION
web*: www.bookjungle.com*
email*: sales@bookjungle.com*
fax*: 630-214-0564*
mail*: Book Jungle PO Box 2226 Champaign, IL 61825*
or PayPal *to sales@bookjungle.com*

Please contact us for bulk discounts

DIRECT-ORDER TERMS
**20% Discount if You Order
Two or More Books**
Free Domestic Shipping!
Accepted: Master Card, Visa,
Discover, American Express

www.ingramcontent.com/pod-product-compliance
Lightning Source LLC
Chambersburg PA
CBHW050353100426
42739CB00015BB/3385